A LEISURE ARTS PUBLICATION

holidays
Remembered

BEST WISHES FOR CHRISTMAS

HALLOWE'EN

LEISURE ARTS, INC.
Little Rock, Arkansas

EDITORIAL STAFF

Editor: Anne Van Wagner Childs. *Executive Director:* Sandra Graham Case. *Creative Art Director:* Gloria Bearden. *Executive Editor:* Susan Frantz Wiles. PRODUCTION — *Managing Editor:* Carla Bentley. *Senior Editor:* Susan Sullivan. *Project Coordinator:* Christine Street. EDITORIAL — *Associate Editor:* Dorothy Latimer Johnson. *Senior Editorial Writer:* Laurie R. Burleson. *Editorial Assistant:* Linda L. Trimble. *Advertising and Direct Mail Copywriters:* Steven M. Cooper and Marla Shivers. ART — *Production Art Director:* Melinda Stout. *Senior Production Artist:* Martha Jordan. *Chart Production Artists:* Paul Allen, Stephen L. Mooningham, Ashley S. Cole, and Deborah Taylor-Choate. *Photography Stylists:* Sondra Harrison Daniel, Karen Smart Hall, Judith Howington Merritt, Charlisa Erwin Parker, and Christina Tiano. *Typesetters:* Cindy Lumpkin and Stephanie Cordero. *Advertising and Direct Mail Artist:* Linda Lovette.

BUSINESS STAFF

Publisher: Steve Patterson. *Controller:* Tom Siebenmorgen. *Retail Sales Director:* Richard Tignor. *Retail Marketing Director:* Pam Stebbins. *Retail Customer Services Director:* Margaret Sweetin. *Marketing Manager:* Russ Barnett. *Executive Director of Marketing and Circulation:* Guy A. Crossley. *Fulfillment Manager:* Byron L. Taylor. *Print Production:* Nancy Reddick Lister and Laura Lockhart.

CREDITS

PHOTOGRAPHY: Ken West, Larry Pennington, Mark Mathews, and Karen Busick Shirey of Peerless Photography, Little Rock, Arkansas; and Jerry R. Davis of Jerry Davis Photography, Little Rock, Arkansas. COLOR SEPARATIONS: Magna IV Engravers of Little Rock, Arkansas. CUSTOM FRAMING: Nelda and Carlton Newby of Creative Framers, North Little Rock, Arkansas. PHOTO ACCESSORIES: R.D. Keever of Cabot, Arkansas, Civil War memorabilia, pages 28-29.

ABOUT OUR COVER: For many of us, the celebration officially begins when we bring our treasured holiday keepsakes out of storage. For our cover photograph, we recreated a Victorian attic holding a cache of sentimental riches — holiday memorabilia for all the days featured in this book, with each collection in its own old-time box. What a delightful way to preserve the decorations we enjoy each year! Our treasures include an antique Halloween papier mâché jack-o'-lantern candy container, a sheep from an old Christmas Nativity, and holiday postcards from long ago.

International Standard Book Number 0-942237-20-X

INTRODUCTION

From New Year's Day until Christmas, our year is filled with special observances and holiday celebrations. Many of the customs we hold dear were given to us by our forefathers, who brought the folklore of their native lands with them to America. Over the years, we have enriched our festivities by adapting their diverse traditions and making them uniquely our own. Just as our cherished celebrations tie us to those who came before us, the wonderful cross stitch designs in Holidays Remembered also give us a glimpse into their time. These decorations — many of which were adapted from antique postcards and scraps — are destined to become tomorrow's heirlooms, to be brought out with other precious keepsakes year after year. May you be inspired to create your own holiday collections of fine cross stitch decorations, and may every celebration you enjoy this year truly become a holiday to remember!

TABLE OF CONTENTS

New Year's Day

The arrival of the new year has been greeted for centuries with welcoming cheers. At the stroke of midnight on New Year's Eve, laughter reigns as we exchange hugs, kisses, and wishes for health and happiness. For in its infancy, the new year reminds us of the potential of the future, filling us with a delightful sense of hope and expectation on this most promising of holidays.

Chart on page 50

7

Valentine's Day

Dedicated to romance, St. Valentine's Day has always been the favorite holiday of lovers. To express their affection for one another on this special day, sweethearts freely exchange cards, gifts, and other tokens of esteem. These heartfelt declarations of devotion are tender testimonials to the power of love!

Chart on page 54

*Cupids, turtledoves, roses, and hearts — these are the
emblems of love that have adorned valentines throughout the years.
In this beautiful collection, these timeless images have been
captured with needle and thread to create sentimental accents
and accessories, all destined to become tomorrow's treasures.*

Chart on page 55

Charts on pages 52-53

Chart on page 54

Charts on page 51

Will you confess?
Or must I guess,
The love I hope is mine.
My heart is true —
Beats but for you,
My own sweet Valentine.

Chart on page 53

PRESIDENTS' DAY

Revered by young and old alike, George Washington and Abraham Lincoln will ever symbolize this country's proud heritage of independence and freedom. As our first president, Washington guided the colonies through the dark days of the American Revolution. It was Lincoln's leadership in the White House that prevented the Civil War from forever dividing the United States. In recent years, instead of celebrating Lincoln's birthday on February 12 and Washington's birthday on February 22, we honor both on Presidents' Day — the third Monday in February.

Charts on page 56

St. Patrick's Day

Steeped in ancient legends and lore, Ireland is home
not only to leprechauns, fairies, and heroic saints,
but also to many stories and songs about them. One of
the Emerald Isle's most fabled figures is St. Patrick, the
country's patron saint. Honored each year on March 17
in both Ireland and America, he is remembered
for the miracles and good works of a lifetime.
The kind spirit of this beloved saint lives on today in
the gentle words of many traditional Celtic blessings.

Chart on page 57

Easter

One of the most joyous celebrations of the year, Easter embraces both the Resurrection's promise of eternal life and the rebirth we see in nature each spring. This charming collection captures many of the beloved images that make this holiday so special. Today, as in the past, bunnies and chicks, colored eggs, and spring flowers enchant both children and adults at Eastertime.

Chart on pages 58-59

Chart on page 64

On Easter morning what an excitement there is to see what the good little hare has brought! Not only real eggs boiled and colored, but sugar ones too, and often wooden ones that open like boxes, disclosing, perhaps, a pair of new gloves or a bright ribbon. He even sometimes brings hoops and skipping-ropes, and generally his own effigy in dough or candy is found trying to scamper away behind the nest.

— F.E. CORNE

Chart on page 63

20

Charts on page 64

Chart on page 61

Charts on page 60

ᵐay the blossoms of Easter rejoice your eye,
The sunshine of Easter brighten your sky,
May the hope of Easter delight your heart,
The joy of Easter ne'er from you depart.

A Happy Easter
May the day for you
be filled with sunshine
and flowers and
friends.
Greetings.

EASTER
GREETINGS

Charts on pages 61-62

Chart on page 93

24

May Day

Warm, sunny weather and May Day often arrive hand in hand, and we find ourselves enticed outdoors to enjoy the fragrance and beauty of our flower gardens. Fulfilling the season's eternal promise of renewal, each dainty new blossom lifts our spirits. The pretty pansies and violets in this collection are lovely year-round reminders of spring. Drawn with delicate precision, illustrations such as the ones from which these designs were adapted are a wonderful legacy left to us by turn-of-the-century artists. Their timeless tributes to the splendor of spring flowers have been preserved on postcards and scraps, and in the bright, colorful seed catalogs that were so popular then.

Oh, the pretty flowers;
Coming ere the Spring-time,
To tell of sunny hours.

— MARY HOWITT

Charts on pages 94-95

Memorial Day

Celebrated in remembrance of the brave men and women who have given their lives for their country, Memorial Day is observed on the last Monday in May. This special holiday, known as Decoration Day in earlier times, originated during the Civil War, when Southern women scattered spring flowers on the graves of those who had died. Today, we carry on the tradition by placing flowers, flags, and other memorial tributes on loved ones' graves. Adapted from a postcard printed during World War I, this patriotic design represents proud servicemen from five wars: a soldier from the American Revolution, a Marine from the War of 1812, a Rebel and a Yankee from the Civil War, a Navy sailor and a Cavalry soldier from the Spanish-American War, and an Army officer from World War I.

One flag, one land,
one heart, one hand,
One Nation, "Evermore!"

Independence Day

The most patriotic of American holidays, Independence Day is a star-spangled celebration of our country's proud heritage of freedom. On this our nation's birthday, spirited citizens have been gathering for generations to send up three cheers for the red, white, and blue. The fun and fellowship we share during the Fourth of July festivities are a tribute to the traditions and ideals of the land that we love!

Charts on pages

halloween

On Halloween, the eve of All Saints' Day, ghosts and other spirits were once believed to roam about, their paths illuminated by the light of glowing jack-o'-lanterns. As superstitions weakened over the centuries, these goblins took on a more playful look, inspiring frightfully delightful postcard art such as that from which these designs were adapted.

Charts on page 72

When the Owl
& Witch
together are seen,
there's mischief brewing
on Hallowe'en.

Chart on pages 70-71

In times gone by, people gathered for reassurance on this bewitching night. They passed the evening by telling ghost stories, bobbing for apples, and playing other games. Today, the spooky parties, frightful decorations, and scary costumes that we so enjoy all reflect the superstitious origins of this haunting holiday.

Charts on page 72

Charts on pages 76-77

Charts on pages 73 and 76-77

Charts on pages 76-77

Chart on page 75

36

To scare away the frightening spirits that they believed were out on Halloween, our ancestors in Ireland donned terrifying costumes and masks. By the time the custom was introduced to Americans by Irish immigrants, it had become a fun-filled opportunity for people to indulge their imaginations. Today, masquerading remains a popular tradition on October 31.

On Hallowe'en
look out!
Strange things are
all about!

Charts on pages 73-74

37

Thanksgiving

Celebrated by the Pilgrims in 1621, the earliest American Thanksgiving was truly an occasion for rejoicing. After a difficult first winter in the New World, they were blessed with a bountiful harvest the following summer and fall. So these thankful settlers set aside a special day of prayer and feasting to express their gratitude. The pleasant custom was repeated year after year, and today, just as the Pilgrims did so long ago, we still give thanks for the blessings in our own lives on Thanksgiving Day, the fourth Thursday in November.

Chart on pages 78-79

Chart on pages 82-83

40

*f*amily and friends are one of life's greatest gifts, and sharing
our Thanksgiving celebrations with those we love is one of the day's
greatest delights. Your guests will be charmed by this serving tray
featuring a plump turkey — one of the traditional symbols of this
American holiday. Adorned with autumn motifs in rich harvest colors,
an afghan draped invitingly across the sofa will tempt your company
to linger a few moments longer as the day's festivities end.

Chart on page 81

*f*or the Pilgrims, the arrival of a ship from Europe was always greeted with sighs of relief and prayers of thanks. Besides delivering precious supplies, the ships sometimes carried beloved friends coming to join them in America. We can just imagine the festivities that were held to honor the newcomers and to rejoice for the provisions they brought with them! In the spirit of the settlers' joyous celebrations, a table set for guests is graced by linen accessories featuring bountiful fruit and vegetable motifs.

Chart on page 80

Chart on pages 82-83

Christmas

Each December as we retell the Christmas story, we are reminded of the divine role played by angels. With their jubilant message of "Peace on earth, good will toward men," these celestial beings were the first to herald the birth of the Baby Jesus. This elegant collection honors the sweet souls sent from heaven with glad tidings of hope, joy, and love.

Charts on pages 86-87

Chart on pages 84-85

46

Capturing the innocence and purity of angels as we imagine them to be, these lovely designs make glorious Yuletide decorations. With their flowing robes, graceful wings, and gentle expressions, the angels here bear cherished symbols of the Christmas story.

Charts on pages 88-91

Chart on page 87

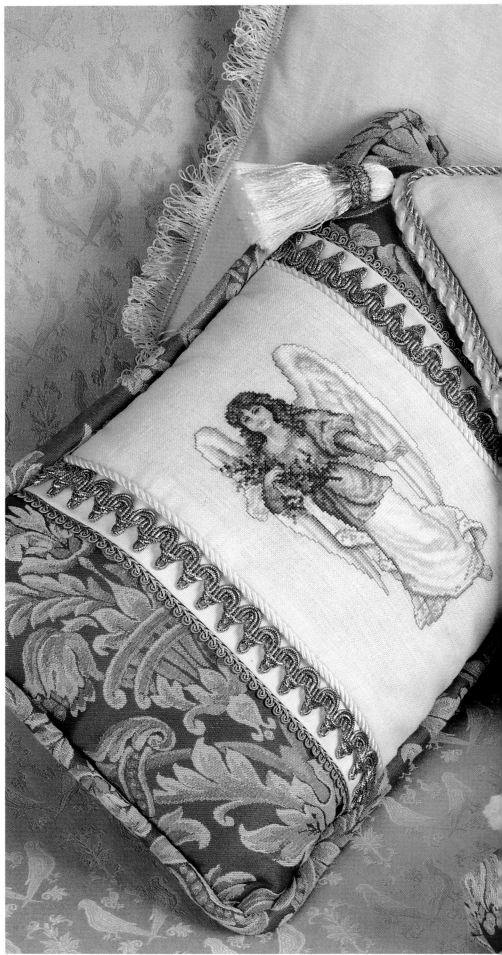

Good news from heaven
    the angels bring
Glad tidings to the earth
    they sing:
To us this day a child
    is given,
To crown us with the joy
    of heaven.

— MARTIN LUTHER

Charts on pages 84-85, 88-91

New Year's Day

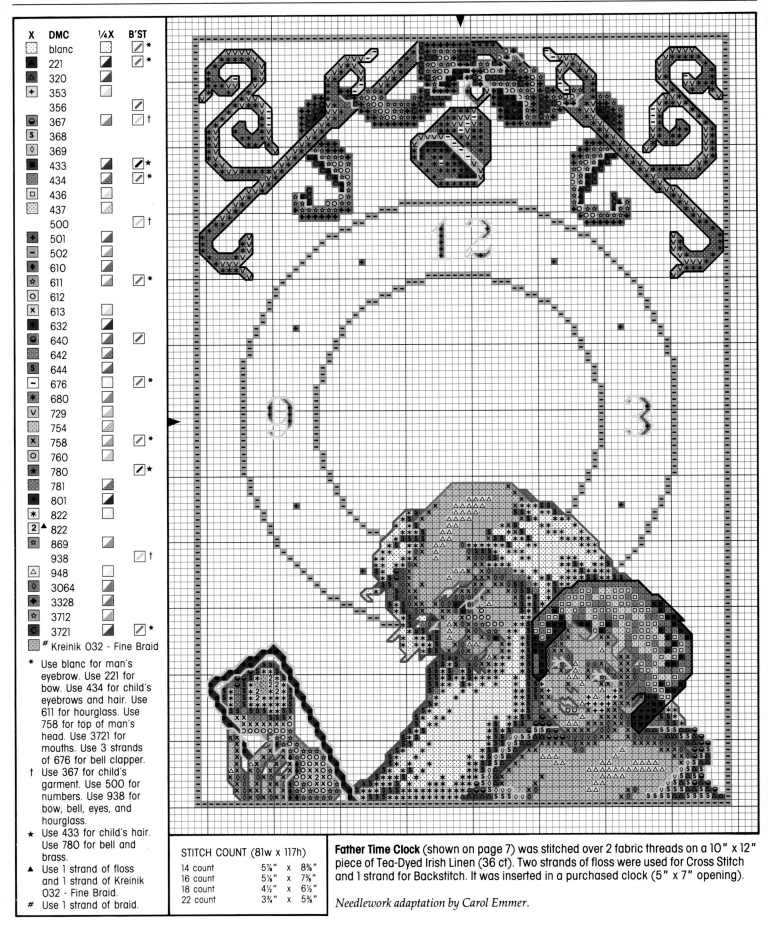

X	DMC	¼X	B'ST
	blanc		*
	221		*
	320		
	353		
	356		
	367		†
	368		
	369		
	433		★
	434		*
	436		
	437		
	500		†
	501		
	502		
	610		
	611		*
	612		
	613		
	632		
	640		
	642		
	644		
	676		*
	680		
	729		
	754		
	758		*
	760		
	780		★
	781		
	801		
	822		
2	822		
	869		
	938		†
	948		
	3064		
	3328		
	3712		
C	3721		*
	# Kreinik 032 - Fine Braid		

* Use blanc for man's
  eyebrow. Use 221 for
  bow. Use 434 for child's
  eyebrows and hair. Use
  611 for hourglass. Use
  758 for top of man's
  head. Use 3721 for
  mouths. Use 3 strands
  of 676 for bell clapper.

† Use 367 for child's
  garment. Use 500 for
  numbers. Use 938 for
  bow, bell, eyes, and
  hourglass.

★ Use 433 for child's hair.
  Use 780 for bell and
  brass.

▲ Use 1 strand of floss
  and 1 strand of Kreinik
  032 - Fine Braid.

Use 1 strand of braid.

STITCH COUNT (81w x 117h)

14 count	5⅞"	x 8⅜"
16 count	5⅛"	x 7⅜"
18 count	4½"	x 6½"
22 count	3¾"	x 5⅜"

Father Time Clock (shown on page 7) was stitched over 2 fabric threads on a 10" x 12" piece of Tea-Dyed Irish Linen (36 ct). Two strands of floss were used for Cross Stitch and 1 strand for Backstitch. It was inserted in a purchased clock (5" x 7" opening).

Needlework adaptation by Carol Emmer.

Valentine's Day

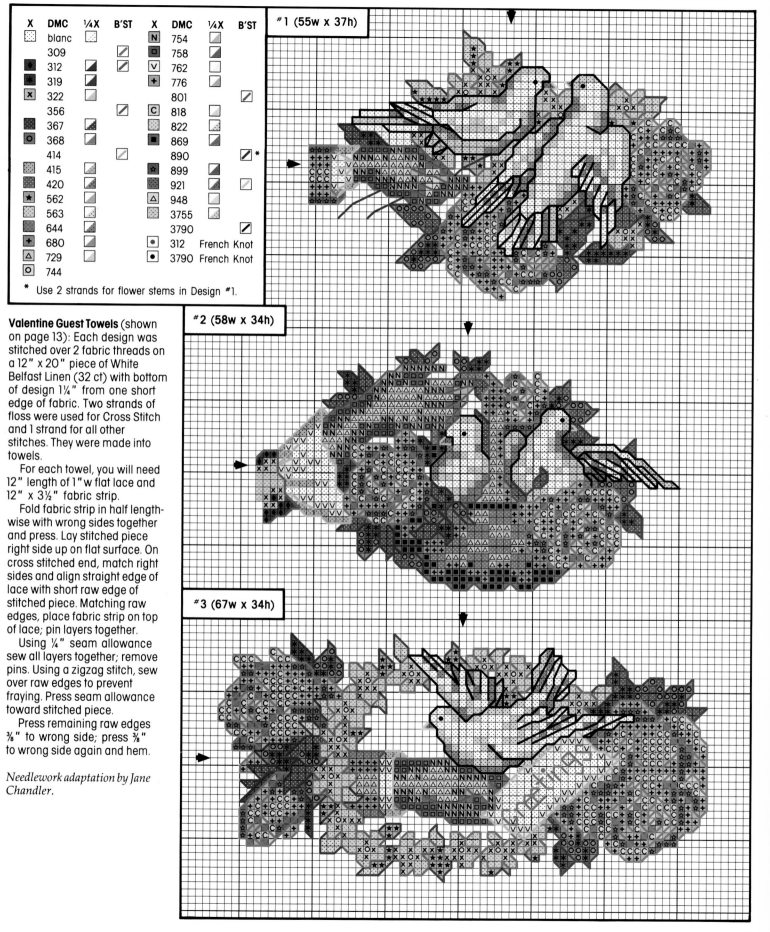

X	DMC	¼X	B'ST		X	DMC	¼X	B'ST
	blanc				N	754		
	309		∕			758		
◆	312		∕		V	762		
✳	319				+	776		
X	322					801		∕
	356		∕		C	818		
	367					822		
O	368					869		
	414		∕			890		∕ *
	415				✩	899		
	420					921		∕
★	562				△	948		
	563					3755		
	644					3790		∕
+	680				●	312	French Knot	
△	729				●	3790	French Knot	
O	744							

* Use 2 strands for flower stems in Design #1.

Valentine Guest Towels (shown on page 13): Each design was stitched over 2 fabric threads on a 12" x 20" piece of White Belfast Linen (32 ct) with bottom of design 1¼" from one short edge of fabric. Two strands of floss were used for Cross Stitch and 1 strand for all other stitches. They were made into towels.

For each towel, you will need 12" length of 1"w flat lace and 12" x 3½" fabric strip.

Fold fabric strip in half lengthwise with wrong sides together and press. Lay stitched piece right side up on flat surface. On cross stitched end, match right sides and align straight edge of lace with short raw edge of stitched piece. Matching raw edges, place fabric strip on top of lace; pin layers together.

Using ¼" seam allowance sew all layers together; remove pins. Using a zigzag stitch, sew over raw edges to prevent fraying. Press seam allowance toward stitched piece.

Press remaining raw edges ⅜" to wrong side; press ⅜" to wrong side again and hem.

Needlework adaptation by Jane Chandler.

#1 (55w x 37h)

#2 (58w x 34h)

#3 (67w x 34h)

Valentine's Day

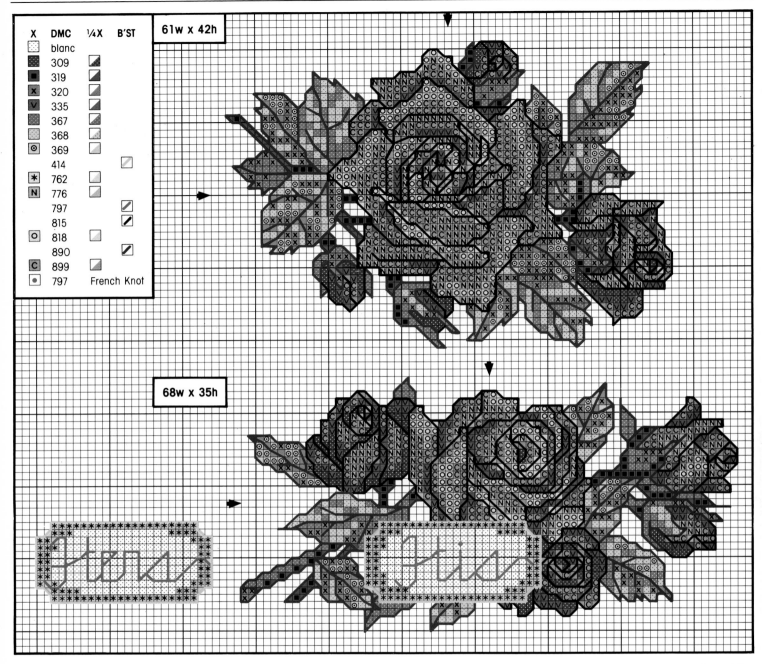

X	DMC	¼X	B'ST	
	blanc			
	309	◢		
■	319	◢		
✕	320	◢		
▼	335	◢		
	367	◢		
	368	◢		
⊙	369	◢		
	414		◢	
✳	762	◢		
N	776	◢		
	797		◢	
	815		◢	
O	818	◢		
	890		◢	
C	899	◢		
•	797			French Knot

61w x 42h

68w x 35h

Rose Sheet (shown on page 11): The design was stitched over a 7½" x 5" piece of 13 mesh waste canvas centered on the band of a bed sheet. Three strands of floss were used for Cross Stitch and 1 strand for Backstitch.

His and Hers Pillowcases (shown on page 11): The design was stitched over an 8" x 5" piece of 13 mesh waste canvas centered on the band of a pillowcase. Three strands of floss were used for Cross Stitch, 2 strands for Backstitch words and French Knot, and 1 strand for all other Backstitch.

Needlework adaptation by Jane Chandler.

WORKING ON WASTE CANVAS

Waste canvas is a special canvas that provides an evenweave grid for placing stitches on fabric. After the design is worked over the canvas, the canvas threads are removed leaving the design on the fabric. The canvas is available in several mesh sizes.

Cover edges of canvas with masking tape. (For sweater, cut a piece of lightweight, non-fusible interfacing the same size as canvas to provide a firm stitching base.)

Find desired stitching area and mark center of area with a pin. Match center of canvas to pin. Use the blue threads in canvas to place canvas straight on project; pin canvas to project. (Pin interfacing to wrong side of sweater.) Baste all thicknesses together as shown in **Fig. 1**.

For sweater, place in a screw type hoop. We recommend a hoop that is large enough to encircle entire design.

Using a sharp needle, work design, stitching from large holes to large holes. Trim canvas to within ¾" of design. Dampen canvas until it becomes limp. Pull out canvas threads one at a time using tweezers (**Fig. 2**). Trim interfacing close to design.

Fig. 1

Fig. 2

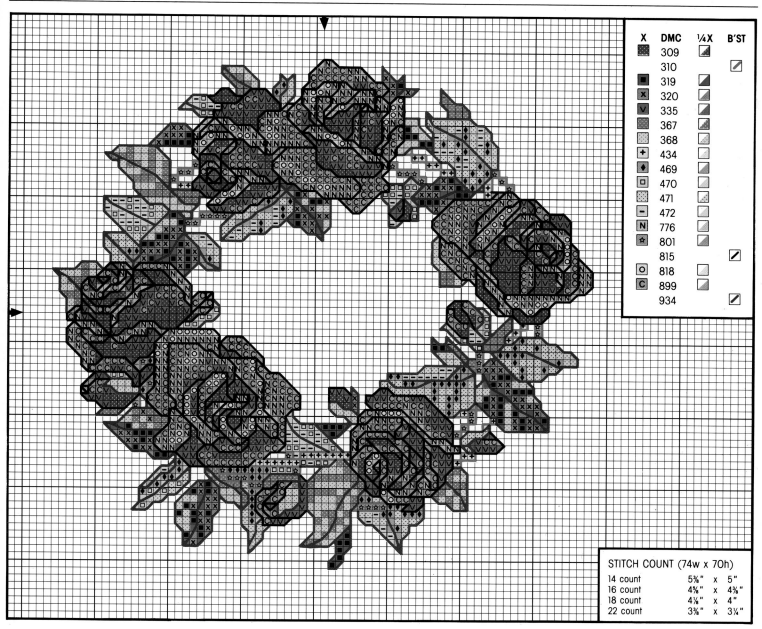

X	DMC	1/4X	B'ST
309			
	310		✓
319			
X	320		
V	335		
367			
368			
+	434		
◆	469		
□	470		
471			
-	472		
N	776		
★	801		
	815		✓
O	818		
C	899		
	934		✓

STITCH COUNT (74w x 70h)

14 count	5⅜"	x	5"
16 count	4⅝"	x	4⅜"
18 count	4⅛"	x	4"
22 count	3⅜"	x	3¼"

Rose Wreath Sweater (shown on page 13): The design was stitched over a 10" square of 12 mesh waste canvas on a purchased sweater. Three strands of floss were used for Cross Stitch, and 1 strand for Backstitch. (See Working on Waste Canvas, page 52.)

Rose Wreath Pillow (shown on page 11): The design was stitched over 2 fabric threads on a 12" square of White Lugana (25 ct). Three strands of floss were used for Cross Stitch and 1 strand for Backstitch.

For pillow, center design and trim stitched piece to measure 10" square. You will also need 10" square of desired fabric for pillow back, 80" length of 2¾"w flat lace, 80" x 6" strip of fabric for ruffle (pieced as necessary), 2" x 42" bias strip of coordinating fabric for cording, 42" length of ¼" dia. purchased cord, and polyester fiberfill.

PILLOW FINISHING

Center cord on wrong side of bias strip; matching long edges, fold strip over cord. Using zipper foot, baste along length of strip close to cord; trim seam allowance to ½". Matching raw edges, pin cording to right side of stitched piece making a ⅜" clip in seam allowance of cording as needed at curves and corners. Ends of cording should overlap approximately 2"; pin overlapping end out of the way. Starting 2" from beginning end of cording and ending 4" from overlapping end, baste cording to stitched piece. On overlapping end of cording, remove 2½" of basting; fold end of fabric back and trim cord so that it meets beginning end of cord. Fold end of fabric under ½"; wrap fabric over beginning end of cording. Finish basting cording to stitched piece.

For fabric and lace ruffle, press short ends of fabric strip ½" to wrong side. Matching wrong sides and long edges, fold strip in half; press. Press short ends of lace ½" to wrong side. Matching raw edge of fabric strip and straight edge of lace, baste layers together close to raw edges. Gather to fit stitched piece. Matching raw edges, pin ruffle to right side of stitched piece overlapping short ends ¼". Using zipper foot and a ½" seam allowance, sew ruffle to stitched piece; remove pins.

Matching right sides and leaving an opening for turning use a ½" seam allowance to sew stitched piece and backing fabric together. Trim seam allowances and clip curves as needed; turn pillow right side out. Stuff pillow with polyester fiberfill and whipstitch opening closed.

Valentine's Day

	STITCH COUNT (88w x 60h)	
14 count	6⅜"	x 4⅜"
16 count	5½"	x 3¾"
18 count	5"	x 3⅜"
22 count	4"	x 2¾"

X	DMC	¼X	B'ST
	blanc		
	ecru		
★	309		/
	310		/
	311		/
◆	312		
–	319		
	320		
	322		
☆	335		
▲	367		
◉	368		
□	369		
★	420		
x	422		
v	642		
	644		
◉	729		
△	776		
	801		/
	815		/
◇	818		
–	822		
✳	869		
	890		/
	899		
◉	3045		
◉	3325		
x	3755		
	3790		/

Doves and Roses Pillow (shown on page 9): The design was stitched on a 12" x 10" piece of White Aida (14 ct). Three strands of floss were used for Cross Stitch and 1 strand for Backstitch.

For pillow, you will need tracing paper, 12" x 10" piece of fabric for pillow backing, 48" length of 1¾"w flat lace, 48" x 4" strip of fabric for ruffle (pieced as necessary), 2" x 25" bias strip of coordinating fabric for cording, 25" length of ¼" dia. purchased cord, and polyester fiberfill.

Fold tracing paper in half and match fold to dashed line of heart pattern. Trace pattern onto tracing paper. Leaving paper folded, cut out pattern. Unfold pattern and press flat. With right sides facing and matching raw edges, place stitched piece and backing fabric together. Center pattern on wrong side of stitched piece. Cut out fabric pieces ½" larger than pattern on all sides.

Complete pillow following Pillow Finishing instructions, page 53.

Doves and Roses Keepsake Box (shown on page 12): The design was stitched over 2 fabric threads on a 14" square of White Lugana (25 ct). Three strands of floss were used for Cross Stitch and 1 strand for Backstitch.

Amounts of the following supplies will be determined by size of box. See instructions for determining amounts. You will need a heart-shaped candy box (our box was approx. 9½" x 10"), tracing paper, adhesive board, batting,

purchased cord, 2"w bias fabric strip to cover cord, 1"w satin ribbon, 1½"w beaded lace, 16" length of 1½"w satin ribbon for bow, and craft glue.

For pattern, draw around box top on tracing paper; cut out. Draw around pattern on adhesive board; cut out. Pin pattern to batting; cut out and remove pattern. Center pattern over stitched piece and pin in place. Cut stitched piece 1" larger than pattern on all sides; remove pattern. Remove paper from adhesive board and apply batting piece. Center stitched piece right side up on top of batting; smoothly fold and glue edges to back of board, clipping into edges of fabric as needed.

For cording, measure around outside edge of heart-shaped adhesive board and add 2". Cut purchased cord and 2"w bias fabric strip determined measurement. Center cord on wrong side of bias fabric strip; matching long edges, fold strip over cord. Using zipper foot, baste along length of strip close to cord. Referring to photo for placement, glue cording around edge of adhesive board.

Glue 1"w satin ribbon around side of box top. Glue **bead only** of beaded lace around bottom edge of box top. Glue mounted stitched piece to top of box. Tie 1½"w satin ribbon in a bow and trim ends as desired. Refer to photo for placement and glue bow to stitched piece.

Needlework adaptation by Jane Chandler.

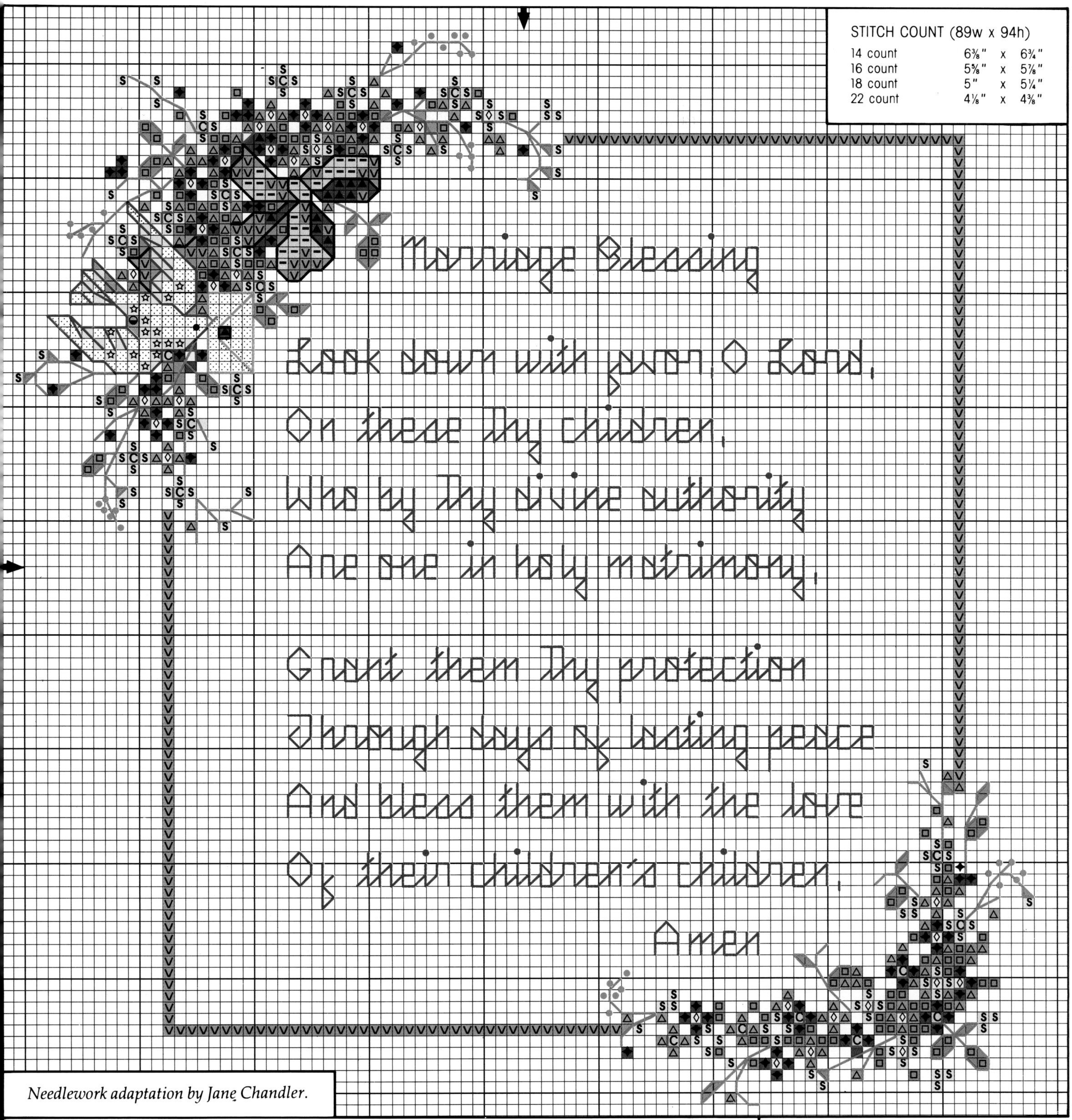
Marriage Blessing
Look down with favor, O Lord,
On these Thy children,
Who by Thy divine authority
Are one in holy matrimony.
Grant them Thy protection
Through days of lasting peace
And bless them with the love
Of their children's children.
Amen

STITCH COUNT (89w x 94h)

14 count	6⅜"	x	6¾"
16 count	5⅝"	x	5⅞"
18 count	5"	x	5¼"
22 count	4⅛"	x	4⅜"

Needlework adaptation by Jane Chandler.

X	DMC	¼X	B'ST	X	DMC	¼X	B'ST	X	DMC	¼X	B'ST	X	DMC	¼X	B'ST
⊡	blanc	⊡		△	518	◪		−	776	◪		●	320	French Knot	
	319		/		535		/		783		/	●	517	French Knot	
□	320	◪			606		/	☆	822	◪		●	3790	French Knot	
	326		/	◒	644	◪		V	899	◪					
▲	335	◪		C	725			S	3761	◪					
◆	517	◪	/	◊	727	◪			3790		/				

Marriage Blessing (shown on page 10): The design was stitched over 2 fabric threads on a 14" square of White Irish Linen (28 ct). Three strands of floss were used for Cross Stitch, 2 strands for Backstitch words, and 1 strand for all other stitches. It was custom framed.

presidents' day

54w x 82h

Abraham Lincoln and George Washington (shown on pages 14-15) were each stitched over 2 fabric threads on an 8" x 10" piece of Antique White Belfast Linen (32 ct). Two strands of floss were used for Cross Stitch and 1 strand for Backstitch. Frames were custom made.

To finish each project you will need tracing paper, cardboard, craft batting, straight pins, hot glue gun and glue sticks, 8" x 12" flag, 8" x 12" piece of white cotton blend fabric, two 8" x 12" pieces of paper-backed fusible web, 14" x 10½" piece of black mat board, 14" x 10½" frame, 20" length of gold cording, and two 6" lengths of gold branches with leaves.

To pad each stitched piece, trace oval pattern (page 96) onto tracing paper; cut out pattern. Draw around pattern on a piece of cardboard; cut out oval. Cut a piece of craft batting same size as cardboard oval. Center pattern over stitched piece; pin in place. Cut out stitched piece 2" larger than pattern. Remove pattern from stitched piece. Center batting, then cardboard on wrong side of stitched piece. Fold edges of stitched piece to back of cardboard and glue in place.

To mount flag on mat board, follow manufacturer's instructions to fuse one piece of paper-backed web to wrong side of flag. Remove paper backing and fuse white fabric to wrong side of flag. Fuse second piece of paper-backed web to white fabric. Remove paper backing and center flag, right side up, on mat board; fuse in place.

Center and glue padded stitched piece to flag. Glue gold cording around edge of stitched piece. Refer to photo for placement of branches and glue in place. Insert in frame.

61w x 80h

X	DMC	¼X	B'ST		X	DMC	¼X	B'ST
	blanc				◇	927		
■	310		✓		◆	934		✓
✳	347	◣	✓			938	◣	✓
○	353				2	3031	◣	✓
◐	356					3328	◣	
◉	520					3363	◣	
△	522				✚	3363		
★	632	◣	✓		▦	3371	◣	◣
	646		✓		C	3768	◣	
	647	◣			−	3770		
☆	648	◣			2	3772	◣	
▲	758					3773	◣	
☆	760				S	3774		
✳	762				V	3778		
✕	839	◣	✓		S	3781	◣	✓
△	840	◣			○	3790		
◆	924	◣			◆	3799	◣	

Needlework adaptation by Donna Vermillion Giampa.

St. patrick's Day

May the most you wish for Be the least you get. May the best times You've ever had Be the worst you will ever see.

OLD CELTIC BLESSING

Designed by Nancy Dockter.

X	DMC	¼X	B'ST		X	DMC	¼X	B'ST
	blanc				△	472		
⊙*	319 & 367					890		⟋
S †	319 & 890					930		⟋★
x	320				⊙	931		
−	368				●	930		French Knot
	414		⟋					
■	469				* Use 1 strand of 319 and 2 strands			
	470				of 367.			
+	471				† Use 2 strands of 319 and 1 strand			
					of 890.			
					★ Use 2 strands for words.			

Celtic Blessing (shown on page 17) was stitched over 2 fabric threads on a 15" x 16" piece of Antique White Dublin Linen (25 ct). Three strands of floss were used for Cross Stitch, 2 strands for Backstitch words and French Knots, and 1 strand for all other Backstitch. It was custom framed.

STITCH COUNT (91w x 98h)	
14 count	6½" x 7"
16 count	5¾" x 6⅛"
18 count	5⅛" x 5½"
22 count	4¼" x 4½"

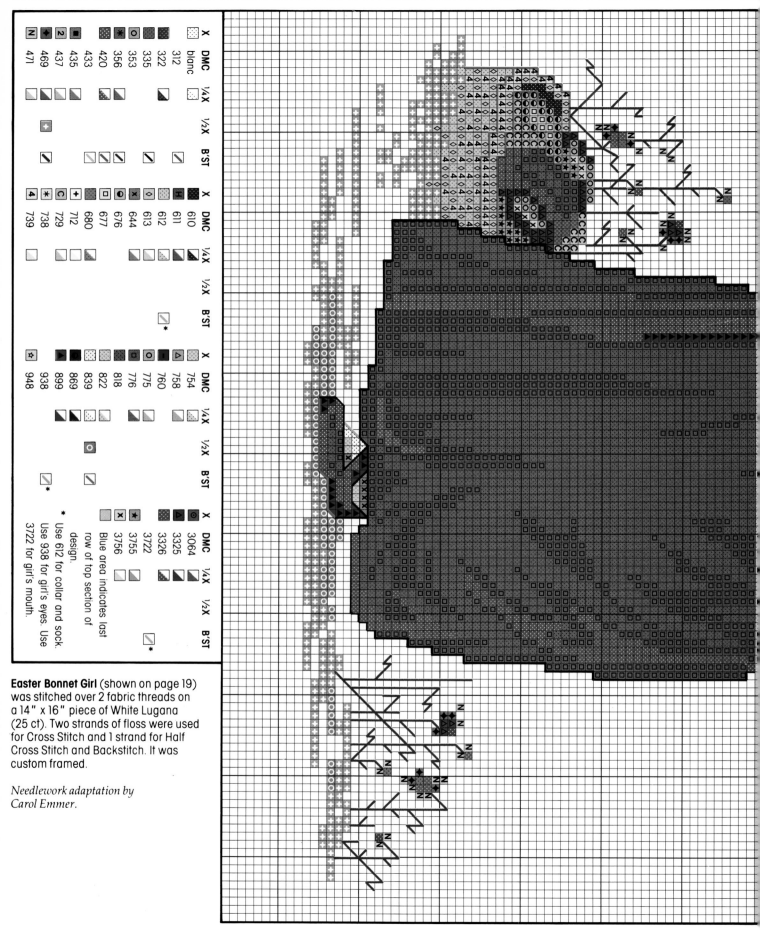

X	¼X	½X	B'ST	DMC
☒				blanc
◆				312
Z			╲	322
■				335
▨				353
✱				356
○				420
▨				433
▨			╲	435
✦		✚	╲	437
▨			╲	469
▨			╲	471

X	¼X	½X	B'ST	DMC
4				610
✱				611
C				612
✚				613
▨				644
□				676
◑				677
✕			╲	680
◇			*	712
▨				729
H				738
■				739

X	¼X	½X	B'ST	DMC
▶				754
■				758
▨				760
▨				775
○		◎		776
I				818
▲				822
✿			╲ *	839
				869
				899
				938
				948

X	¼X	½X	B'ST	DMC
▨	▨			3064
✕				3325
★				3326
▨				3722
▶				3755
◎			╲ *	3756

* Use 612 for top row of design. Blue area indicates last row of top section of design. Use 612 for collar and sock. Use 938 for girl's eyes. Use 3722 for girl's mouth.

Easter Bonnet Girl (shown on page 19) was stitched over 2 fabric threads on a 14" x 16" piece of White Lugana (25 ct). Two strands of floss were used for Cross Stitch and 1 strand for Half Cross Stitch and Backstitch. It was custom framed.

Needlework adaptation by Carol Emmer.

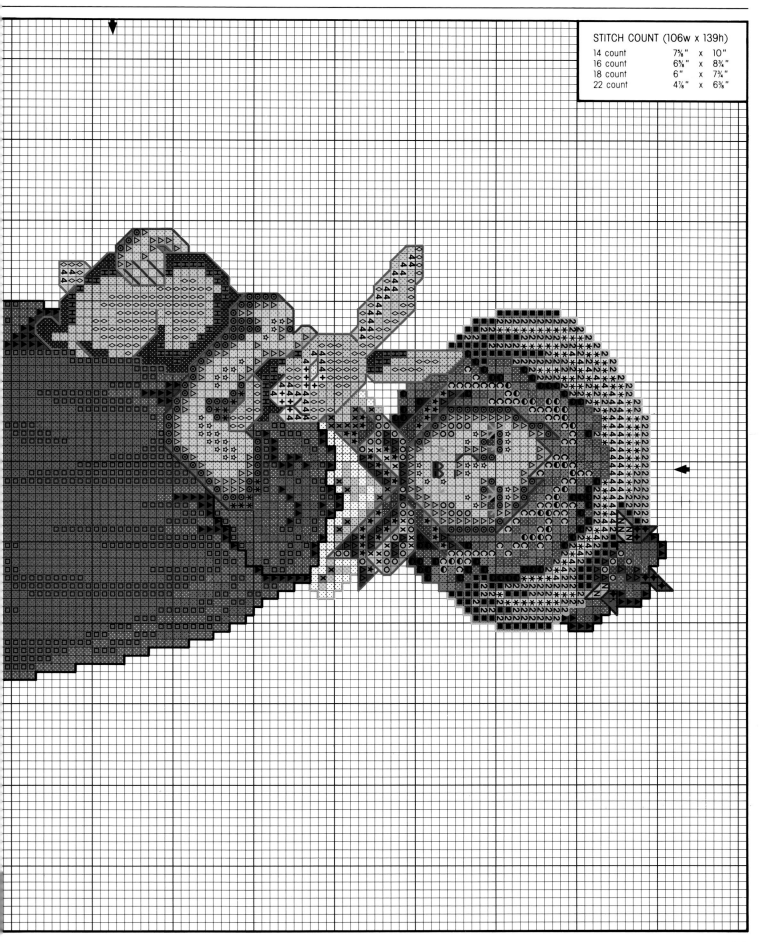

STITCH COUNT (106w x 139h)

count				
14 count	7⅝"	x	10"	
16 count	6⅝"	x	8¾"	
18 count	6"	x	7¾"	
22 count	4⅞"	x	6⅜"	

Easter

Flower Girls (shown on page 22): Each design was stitched on a 6" square of Ivory Aida (18 ct). Two strands of floss were used for Cross Stitch and 1 strand for Backstitch. They were inserted in artificial flowers.

Trace pattern onto tracing paper; cut out pattern. For each Flower Girl, center pattern on right side of stitched piece and draw around pattern; cut out. Thread needle with a 20" length of six-strand embroidery floss and baste ½" from raw edge of stitched piece. Pull ends of floss to gather stitched piece; firmly stuff with polyester fiberfill. Pull floss ends tight and knot to secure. Apply a generous amount of liquid fray preventative to raw edges of stitched piece (up to basting line); allow to dry. Trim raw edges ⅛" from basting line; clip excess floss ends.

If necessary, remove center of artificial flower. Refer to photo and hot glue stitched piece to inside center of flower.

Designed by Carol Emmer.

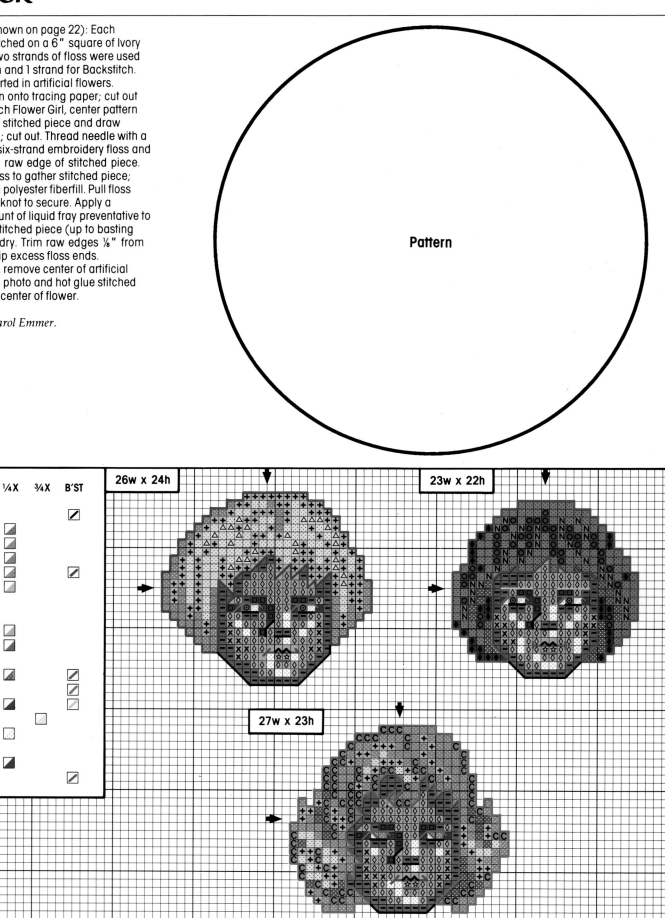

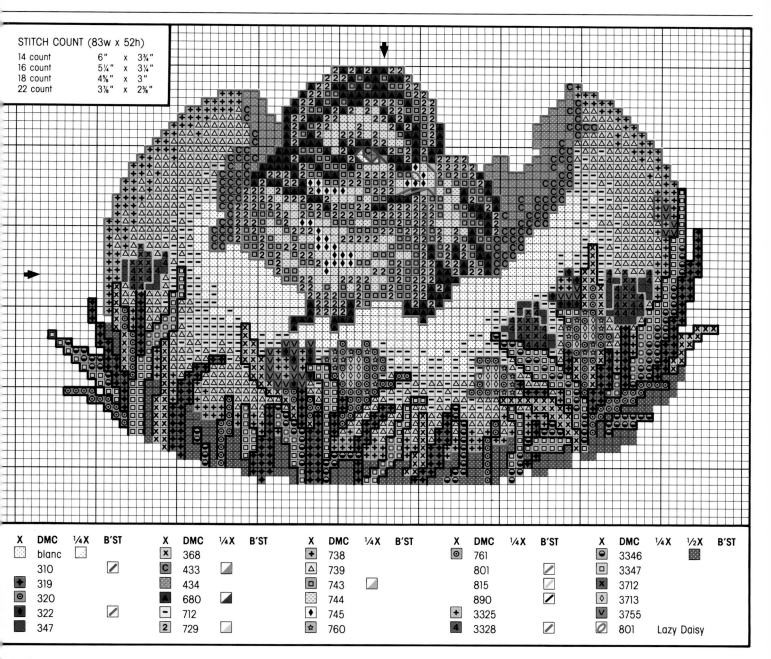

STITCH COUNT (83w x 52h)

14 count	6" x 3¾"
16 count	5¼" x 3¼"
18 count	4⅝" x 3"
22 count	3⅞" x 2⅜"

X	DMC	¼X	B'ST	X	DMC	¼X	B'ST	X	DMC	¼X	B'ST	X	DMC	¼X	B'ST	X	DMC	¼X	½X	B'ST
	blanc			×	368			+	738			⊙	761			●	3346			
	310			C	433			△	739				801			□	3347			
◆	319				434			◻	743				815			×	3712			
⊙	320			▲	680				744				890			◇	3713			
■	322			-	712			◆	745			+	3325			V	3755			
	347			2	729			☆	760			4	3328			⊘	801		Lazy Daisy	

Chick in Frame (shown on page 21): The design was stitched over 2 fabric threads on a 12" x 10" piece of White Belfast Linen (32 ct). Two strands of floss were used for Cross Stitch and 1 strand for all other stitches. It was custom framed.

Chick Sweater (shown on page 23): The design was stitched over an 11" x 8" piece of 12 mesh waste canvas on a purchased sweater with top of design approx. 1½" below bottom of neckband. Three strands of floss were used for Cross Stitch and 1 strand for all other stitches.

Needlework adaptation by Jane Chandler.

WORKING ON WASTE CANVAS

Waste canvas is a special canvas that provides an evenweave grid for placing stitches on fabric. After the design is worked over the canvas, the canvas threads are removed leaving the design on the fabric. The canvas is available in several mesh sizes.

Cover edges of canvas with masking tape. Cut a piece of lightweight, non-fusible interfacing the same size as canvas to provide a firm stitching base.

Find desired stitching area on sweater and mark center of area with a pin. Match center of canvas to pin. Use the blue threads in canvas to place canvas straight on sweater; pin canvas to sweater. Pin interfacing to wrong side of sweater. Baste all three thicknesses together as shown in **Fig. 1**.

Place sweater in a screw type hoop. We recommend a hoop that is large enough to encircle entire design. Using a sharp needle, work design, stitching from large holes to large holes.

Trim canvas to within ¾" of design. Dampen canvas until it becomes limp. Pull out canvas threads one at a time using tweezers (**Fig. 2**). Trim interfacing close to design.

Fig. 1 **Fig. 2**

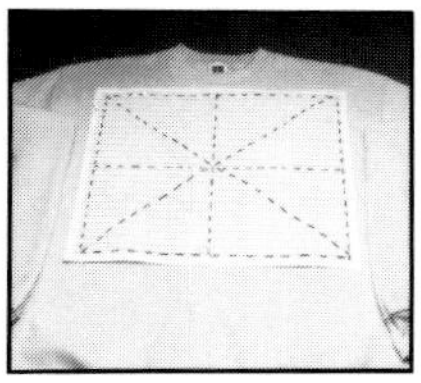

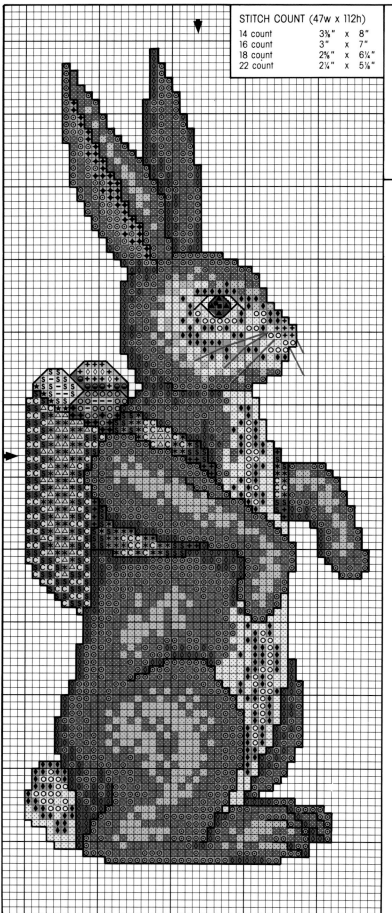

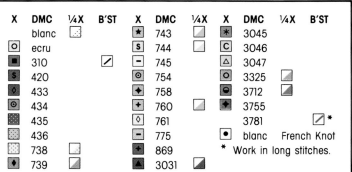

STITCH COUNT (47w x 112h)

14 count	3⅜"	x	8"
16 count	3"	x	7"
18 count	2⅝"	x	6¼"
22 count	2¼"	x	5⅛"

X	DMC	¼X	B'ST	X	DMC	¼X	X	DMC	¼X	B'ST
	blanc	◩		★	743	◩	✱	3045		
o	ecru			S	744	◩	C	3046		
■	310		/	−	745		△	3047		
S	420			⊙	754		O	3325	◩	
◊	433			✦	758		◒	3712	◩	
⊙	434			+	760	◩	✦	3755		
	435			◊	761			3781		/ *
	436			−	775		•	blanc	French Knot	
	738	◩		✦	869		*	Work in long stitches.		
◆	739	◩		▲	3031	◩				

Bunny Figure (shown on page 23): The design was stitched on a 9" x 15" piece of Ivory Aida (11 ct). Four strands of floss were used for Cross Stitch and 2 strands for Backstitch and French Knot. It was made into a stuffed figure.

For stuffed figure, cut a piece of Aida same size as stitched piece for backing. Matching right sides and raw edges and leaving bottom edge open, sew stitched piece and backing fabric together ¼" from design. Trim excess fabric leaving a ¼" seam allowance. Clip seam allowances at curves; turn figure right side out and carefully push curves outward. Trim bottom edge of figure ½" from bottom of design. Press raw edges ¼" to wrong side; stuff figure with polyester fiberfill up to 1½" from opening.

For base, set figure on tracing paper and draw around base of figure. Add a ½" seam allowance to pattern; cut out. Place pattern on a piece of Aida. Use fabric marking pencil to draw around pattern; cut out along drawn line. Baste around base piece ½" from raw edge; press raw edges to wrong side along basting line.

To weight bottom of figure, fill a plastic sandwich bag with a small amount of aquarium gravel. Place bag of gravel into bottom of figure.

Pin wrong side of base piece over opening. Whipstitch in place, adding polyester fiberfill as necessary to fill bottom of figure. Remove basting threads.

Bunny Sweater (shown on page 23): The design was stitched over a 7½" x 13" piece of 11 mesh waste canvas on a purchased cardigan. Four strands of floss were used for Cross Stitch and 2 strands for Backstitch and French Knot. (See Working on Waste Canvas, page 61.)

Designed by Jane Chandler.

Girl and Bunny Hat Box (shown on page 20): The design was stitched over 2 fabric threads on a 14" square of White Lugana (25 ct). Three strands of floss were used for Cross Stitch and 1 strand for Backstitch. It was applied to the lid of a hat box.

For lid, cut a paper pattern 1" larger on all sides than box lid. Centering pattern on design, cut out stitched piece. Clip ⅜" into edge of stitched piece at 1" intervals. Cut batting same size as lid; place batting on lid. Place stitched piece on batting; fold edge of stitched piece down and glue to side of lid. Layer and glue ribbon around side of lid in the following order: ⅞"w satin ribbon, ½"w satin ribbon, and ¼"w grosgrain ribbon.

Needlework adaptation by Carol Emmer.

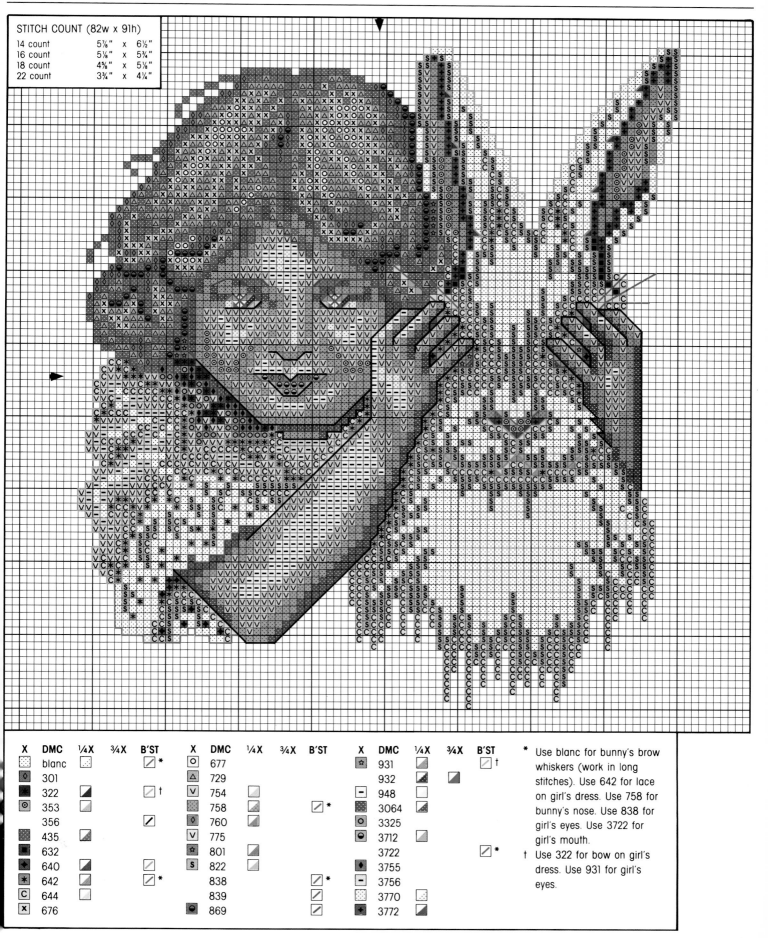

STITCH COUNT (82w x 91h)

14 count	5⅞"	x	6½"
16 count	5⅛"	x	5¾"
18 count	4⅝"	x	5⅛"
22 count	3¾"	x	4¼"

X	DMC	¼X	¾X	B'ST		X	DMC	¼X	¾X	B'ST		X	DMC	¼X	¾X	B'ST
	blanc			⟋*		○	677					☆	931	⟋		⟋ †
◇	301					△	729						932	⟋	⟋	
✳	322	⟋		⟋ †		V	754	⟋				–	948			
⊙	353	⟋					758	⟋		⟋*			3064	⟋		
	356		⟋			◇	760	⟋				○	3325	⟋		
	435	⟋				V	775					◕	3712	⟋		
■	632					☆	801	⟋					3722			⟋*
◆	640	⟋				S	822	⟋				◆	3755	⟋		
✳	642	⟋		⟋*			838			⟋*		–	3756			
C	644	⟋					839		⟋				3770	⟋		
✕	676					◕	869					◆	3772	⟋		

* Use blanc for bunny's brow whiskers (work in long stitches). Use 642 for lace on girl's dress. Use 758 for bunny's nose. Use 838 for girl's eyes. Use 3722 for girl's mouth.

† Use 322 for bow on girl's dress. Use 931 for girl's eyes.

63

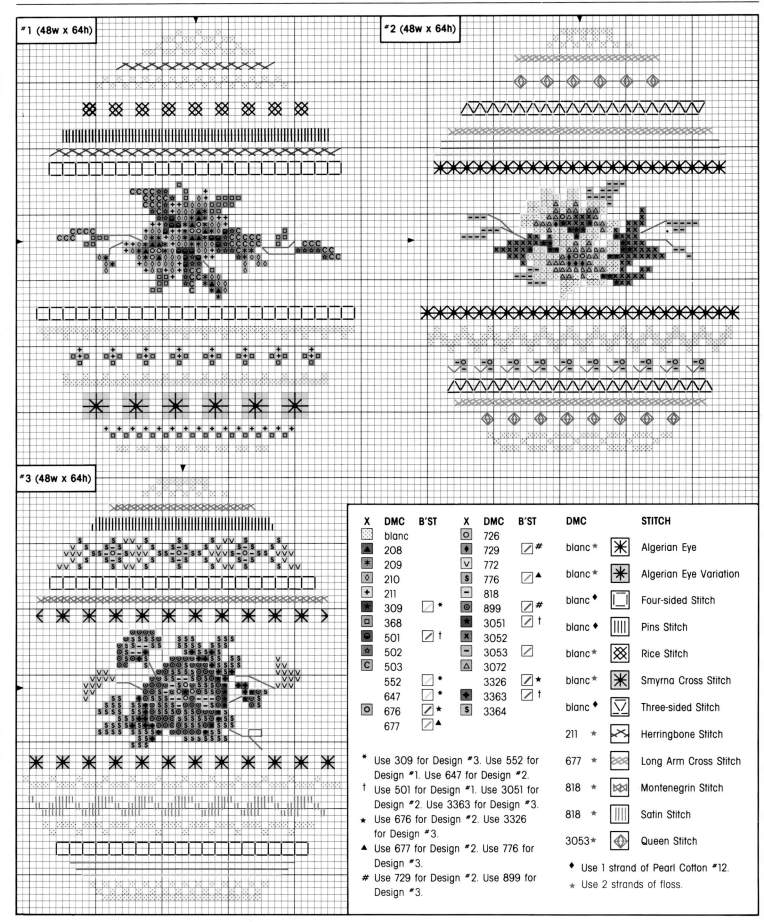

#1 (48w x 64h)

#2 (48w x 64h)

#3 (48w x 64h)

X	DMC	B'ST	X	DMC	B'ST	DMC	STITCH
	blanc			726		blanc ★	Algerian Eye
	208			729	#	blanc ★	Algerian Eye Variation
	209			772		blanc ◆	Four-sided Stitch
	210			776	▲	blanc ◆	Pins Stitch
	211			818		blanc ★	Rice Stitch
	309	*		899	#	blanc ★	Smyrna Cross Stitch
	368			3051	†	blanc ◆	Three-sided Stitch
	501	†		3052		211 ★	Herringbone Stitch
	502			3053		677 ★	Long Arm Cross Stitch
	503			3072		818 ★	Montenegrin Stitch
	552	*		3326	★	818 ★	Satin Stitch
	647	*		3363	†	3053 ★	Queen Stitch
	676	★		3364			
	677	▲					

* Use 309 for Design #3. Use 552 for Design #1. Use 647 for Design #2.

† Use 501 for Design #1. Use 3051 for Design #2. Use 3363 for Design #3.

★ Use 676 for Design #2. Use 3326 for Design #3.

▲ Use 677 for Design #2. Use 776 for Design #3.

Use 729 for Design #2. Use 899 for Design #3.

◆ Use 1 strand of Pearl Cotton #12.

★ Use 2 strands of floss.

Egg Ornaments (shown on page 21): Each design was stitched over 2 fabric threads on a 6" x 8" piece of White Belfast Linen (32 ct). Two strands of floss were used for Cross Stitch and 1 strand for Backstitch. Refer to chart for number of strands to use for Embroidery and Pulled Stitches.

For each ornament, you will need 4" Styrofoam® egg, 6" x 8" piece of Belfast Linen for back, craft glue, T-pins, 18" length of 1"w wire-edged ribbon, 18" length of satin cord, and 13" lengths of the following: ⅛"w satin ribbon, ½"w satin ribbon, and ½"w decorative trim.

Using outside edge of design as guide, trim stitched piece in oval shape ½" larger on all sides than design. Cut backing fabric same size as stitched piece. Apply glue to wrong side of backing fabric and position on egg smoothing wrinkles and easing excess fabric at sides. Stick T-pins into egg around raw edges of fabric to hold in place. Repeat for stitched piece. Remove T-pins when glue has dried. Center and glue trims around egg over raw edges in the following order: ⅛"w ribbon, ½"w ribbon, and ½"w trim.

Use 1"w wire-edged ribbon to make bow. Glue bow to top of ornament. For hanger, glue each end of satin cord to top of ornament behind bow.

Violet Collar Point (shown on page 20): The violet from Design #1 was stitched over a 3" square of 16 mesh waste canvas on the collar point of a purchased blouse. Two strands of floss were used for Cross Stitch and 1 strand for Backstitch. (See Working on Waste Canvas, page 52.)

Designed by Linda Culp Calhoun.

EMBROIDERY STITCHES

(**Note:** For Figs. with numbered stitches, come up at 1 and all odd numbers; go down at 2 and all even numbers.)

Herringbone Stitch: This overlapping stitch is worked continuously from left to right. Complete first stitch (stitches 1-4); then work next stitch (stitches 5-8) as shown in **Fig. 1**. Work all consecutive stitches in the same manner as stitches 5-8.

Fig. 1

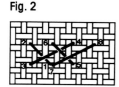

Long Arm Cross Stitch: This overlapping stitch is worked continuously from left to right. Complete first stitch (stitches 1-4); then work next stitch (stitches 5-8) as shown in **Fig. 2**. Work all consecutive stitches in the same manner as stitches 5-8.

Fig. 2

Montenegrin Stitch: This overlapping stitch is worked continuously from left to right. Complete first stitch (stitches 1-6) as shown in **Fig. 3a**; then work next stitch (stitches 7-12) (**Fig. 3b**). Work all consecutive stitches in the same manner as stitches 7-12.

Fig. 3a **Fig. 3b**

Queen Stitch: This decorative stitch forms a diamond shape. Pull a long stitch (stitch 1-2) loosely and catch with a short stitch (stitch 3-4) (**Fig. 4a**). Complete stitch (stitches 5-16), catching each long stitch with a short stitch as shown in **Figs. 4a-c**.

Fig. 4a **Fig. 4b** **Fig. 4c**

Rice Stitch: This decorative stitch is formed by first working a large Cross Stitch (stitches 1-4) and then working a stitch over each leg of the Cross Stitch (stitches 5-12) as shown in **Fig. 5**.

Fig. 5

Satin Stitch: This stitch is a series of straight stitches worked side by side (**Fig. 6**). The number of threads worked over and the direction of stitches will vary according to the chart.

Fig. 6

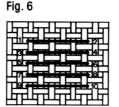

Smyrna Cross Stitch: This decorative stitch is formed by working four stitches (stitches 1-8) as shown in **Fig. 7**. The top stitch (stitch 7-8) of all Smyrna Cross Stitches must be made in the same direction.

Fig. 7

PULLED STITCHES

Fabric threads should be pulled tightly together to create an opening in the fabric around the stitch. Figs. show placement of stitch but do not show pulling of the fabric threads. Keep tension even throughout work.

Algerian Eye Stitch: An "eye" is formed in the center of this stitch. Come up at 1, go down in center, and pull tightly toward 3. Come up at 3, go down in center, and pull tightly toward 5; continue working in this manner until stitch is complete (stitches 5-15) (**Fig. 8**). Work row of Algerian Eye Stitches from right to left.

Fig. 8

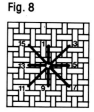

Four-sided Stitch: This continuous stitch is worked from left to right. Come up at 1 and pull tightly toward 2; then go down at 2 and pull tightly toward 1. Work stitches 3-14 in same manner (**Fig. 9**). Continue working in the same manner to end of row.

Fig. 9

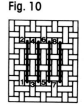

Pins Stitch: This stitch is a series of straight stitches worked side by side (**Fig. 10**). Complete stitch 1-2, come up at 3, and pull tightly; go down at 4, come up at 5, and pull tightly. Continue working in the same manner to end of row.

Fig. 10

Three-sided Stitch: This continuous stitch is worked from right to left. Each stitch is worked twice; stitches 1-2 and 3-4 are over the same fabric threads (**Fig. 11a**). Come up at 1 and pull tightly toward 2; then go down at 2 and pull tightly toward 1. Work stitch 3-4 over the same fabric threads. Work stitches 5-22 in same manner (**Figs. 11a-c**). Continue working in the same manner to end of row.

Fig. 11a **Fig. 11b**

Fig. 11c

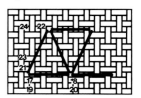

Memorial Day

X	DMC	¼X	B'ST
	blanc		
	311		
	312		
	319		
	321		
	322		
	336		
	347		
	356		
	367		
C	368		
	420		
	422		
	433		
	434		
	498		
	632		
	640		
S	642		
	644		
	645		
2	646		
	647		
V	648		
	676		
−	677		
	680		
	729		
	754		
	758		
	801		
S	815		
	822		
	823		
−	844		
	869		
	898		
	930		
S	931		
−	932		
X	948		
	3045		
	3046		
	3047		
	3064		
X	3072		
	3371		
	3712		
	3750		

Purple area indicates last row of right section of design.

Memorial Day Soliders (shown on page 29) was stitched over 2 fabric threads on a 16" x 13" piece of Antique White Belfast Linen (32 ct). Two strands of floss were used for Cross Stitch and 1 strand for Backstitch. It was custom framed.

Needlework adaptation by Carol Emmer.

STITCH COUNT (161w x 114h)

14 count	11½"	x	8¼"
16 count	10⅛"	x	7⅛"
18 count	9"	x	6⅜"
22 count	7⅜"	x	5¼"

One flag, one Land,
one heart, one hand,
One Nation, "Evermore!"

Independence Day

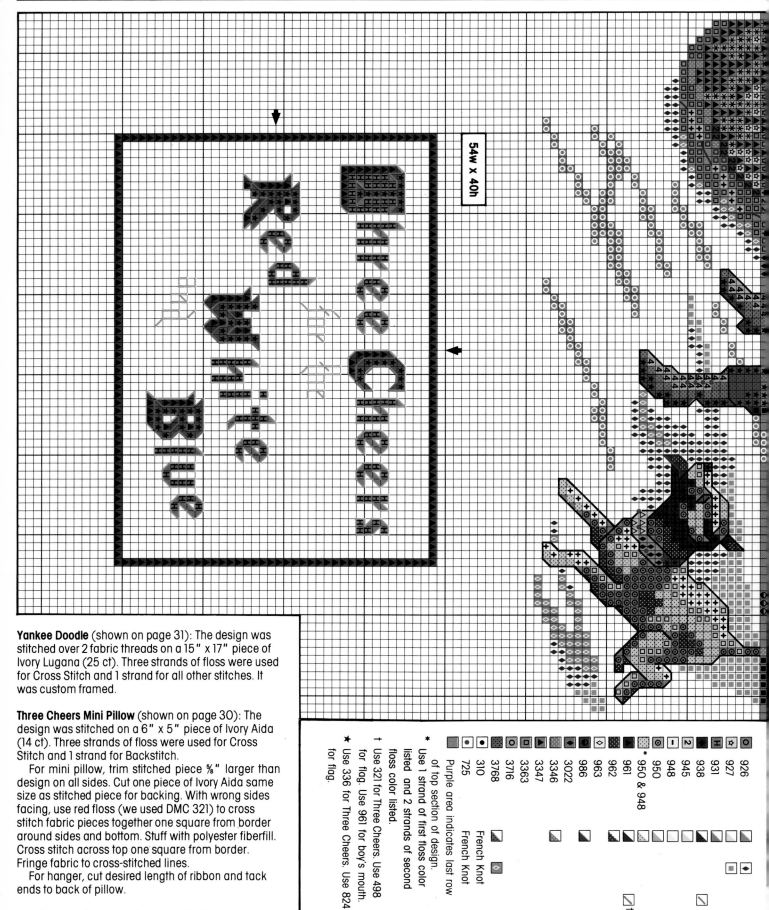

54w x 40h

Yankee Doodle (shown on page 31): The design was stitched over 2 fabric threads on a 15" x 17" piece of Ivory Lugana (25 ct). Three strands of floss were used for Cross Stitch and 1 strand for all other stitches. It was custom framed.

Three Cheers Mini Pillow (shown on page 30): The design was stitched on a 6" x 5" piece of Ivory Aida (14 ct). Three strands of floss were used for Cross Stitch and 1 strand for Backstitch.

For mini pillow, trim stitched piece ⅝" larger than design on all sides. Cut one piece of Ivory Aida same size as stitched piece for backing. With wrong sides facing, use red floss (we used DMC 321) to cross stitch fabric pieces together one square from border around sides and bottom. Stuff with polyester fiberfill. Cross stitch across top one square from border. Fringe fabric to cross-stitched lines.

For hanger, cut desired length of ribbon and tack ends to back of pillow.

Needlework adaptations by Nancy Dockter.

	926
	927
	931
	938
	945
	948
	950
	950 & 948
	961
	962
	963
	986
	3022
	3346
	3347
	3363
	3716
	3768
	310
	725

French Knot
French Knot

* Purple area indicates last row of top section of design.
* Use 1 strand of first floss color listed and 2 strands of second floss color listed.
† Use 321 for Three Cheers. Use 498 for flag. Use 961 for boy's mouth.
★ Use 336 for Three Cheers. Use 824 for flag.

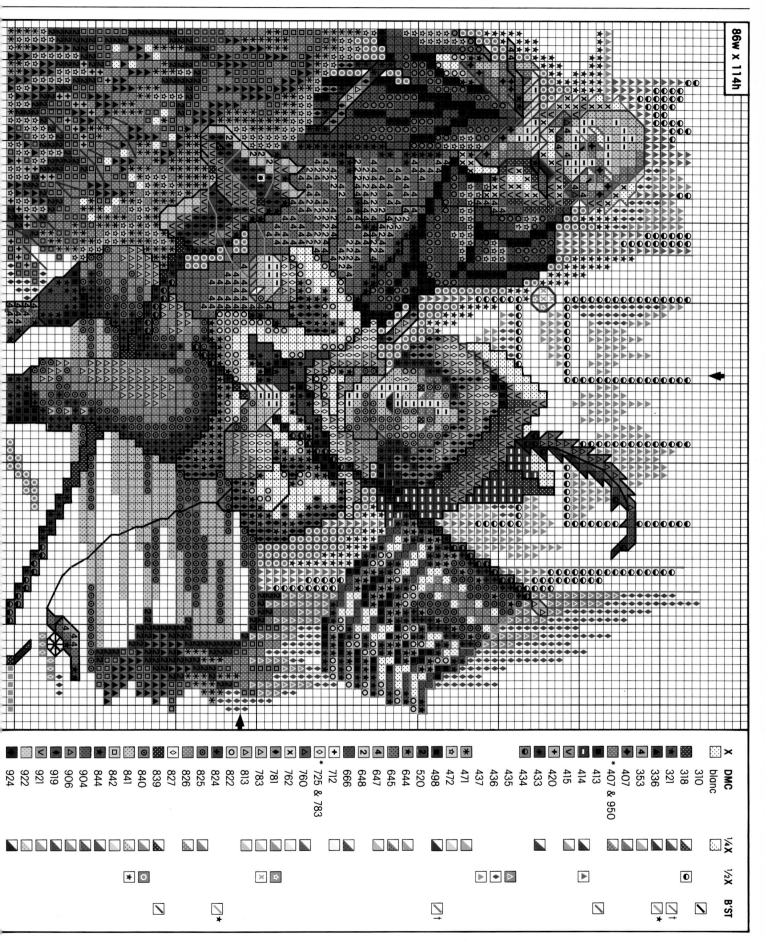

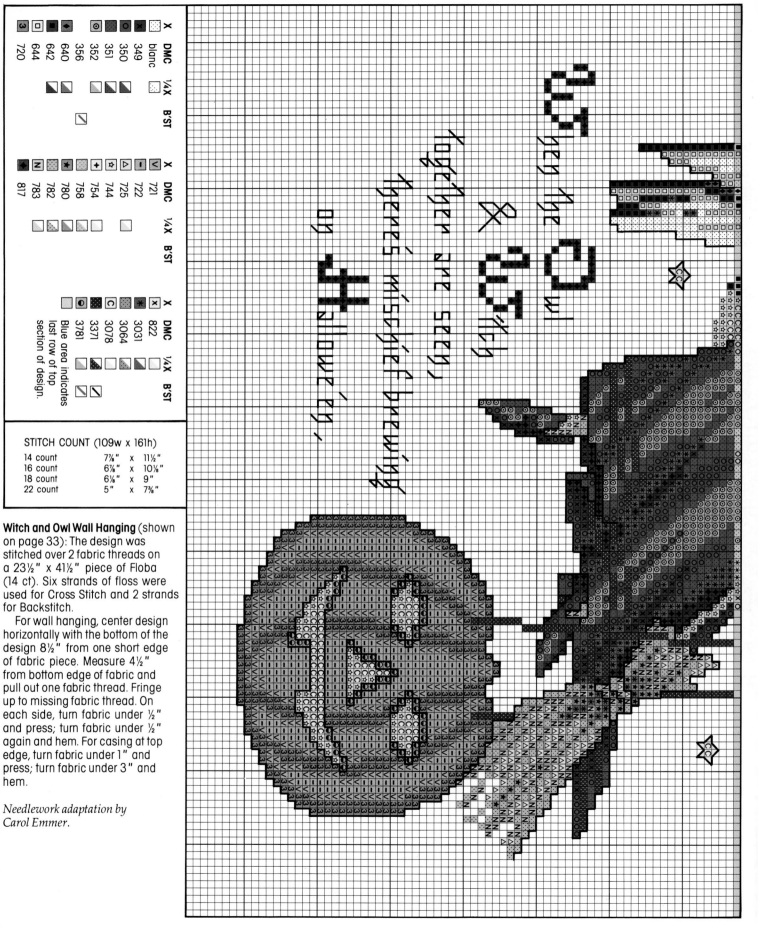

3	□	■	◆		⊙	■	⊙	☒	·::	X
720	644	642	640	356	352	351	350	349	blanc	DMC
										¼X
			◪	◪		◪	◪	◪		B'ST
							◲			

◆	N	□	★	+	✿	▷	I	<	X
817	783	782	780	758	754	744	725	722	721	DMC
										¼X
◪	◪	◪		◪						B'ST

▨	◑	▦	C	▨	✳	☒	X
3781	3371	3078	3064	3031	822	DMC
						¼X
◪	◪	◪	◪	◪		B'ST
◲	◲					

Blue area indicates
last row of top
section of design.

STITCH COUNT (109w x 161h)

14 count	7⅞"	x	11½"
16 count	6⅞"	x	10⅛"
18 count	6⅛"	x	9"
22 count	5"	x	7⅞"

Witch and Owl Wall Hanging (shown on page 33): The design was stitched over 2 fabric threads on a 23½" x 41½" piece of Floba (14 ct). Six strands of floss were used for Cross Stitch and 2 strands for Backstitch.

For wall hanging, center design horizontally with the bottom of the design 8½" from one short edge of fabric piece. Measure 4½" from bottom edge of fabric and pull out one fabric thread. Fringe up to missing fabric thread. On each side, turn fabric under ½" and press; turn fabric under ½" again and press. For casing at top edge, turn fabric under 1" and press; turn fabric under 3" and hem.

Needlework adaptation by Carol Emmer.

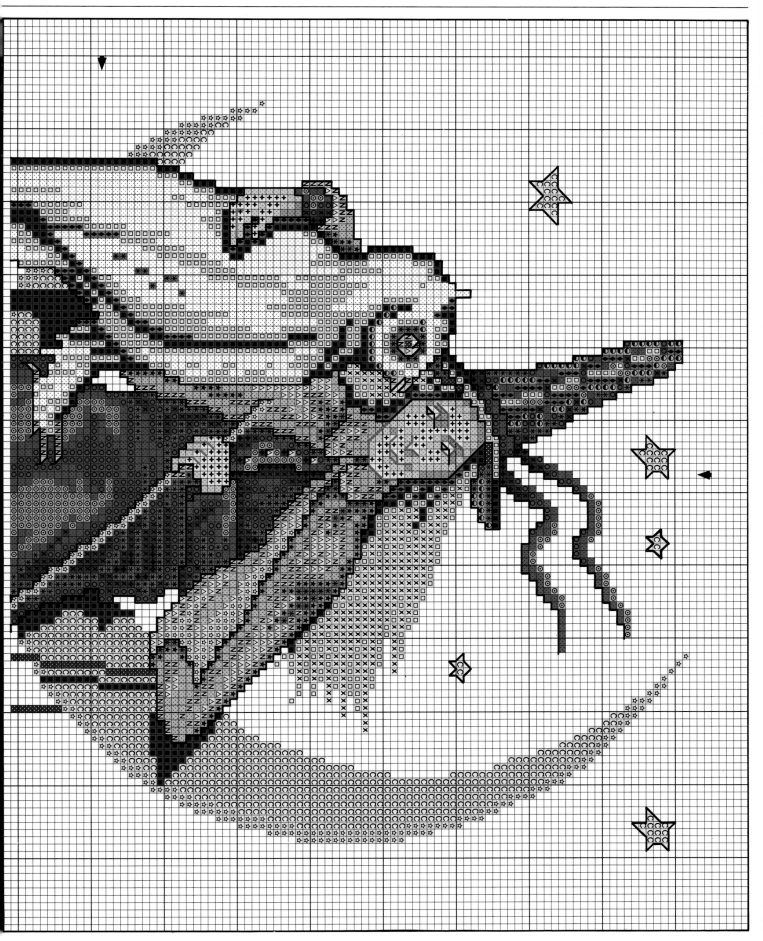

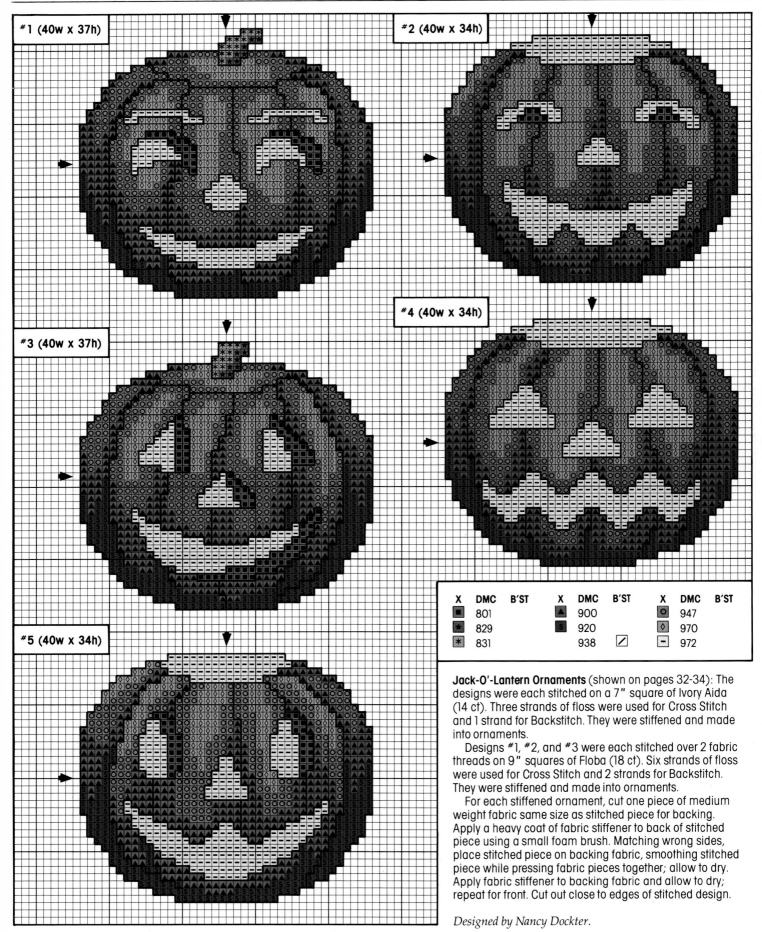

#1 (40w x 37h)

#2 (40w x 34h)

#4 (40w x 34h)

#3 (40w x 37h)

#5 (40w x 34h)

X	DMC	B'ST	X	DMC	B'ST	X	DMC	B'ST
■	801		▲	900		◉	947	
★	829		S	920		◈	970	
✳	831			938	╱	⊟	972	

Jack-O'-Lantern Ornaments (shown on pages 32-34): The designs were each stitched on a 7" square of Ivory Aida (14 ct). Three strands of floss were used for Cross Stitch and 1 strand for Backstitch. They were stiffened and made into ornaments.

Designs #1, #2, and #3 were each stitched over 2 fabric threads on 9" squares of Floba (18 ct). Six strands of floss were used for Cross Stitch and 2 strands for Backstitch. They were stiffened and made into ornaments.

For each stiffened ornament, cut one piece of medium weight fabric same size as stitched piece for backing. Apply a heavy coat of fabric stiffener to back of stitched piece using a small foam brush. Matching wrong sides, place stitched piece on backing fabric, smoothing stitched piece while pressing fabric pieces together; allow to dry. Apply fabric stiffener to backing fabric and allow to dry; repeat for front. Cut out close to edges of stitched design.

Designed by Nancy Dockter.

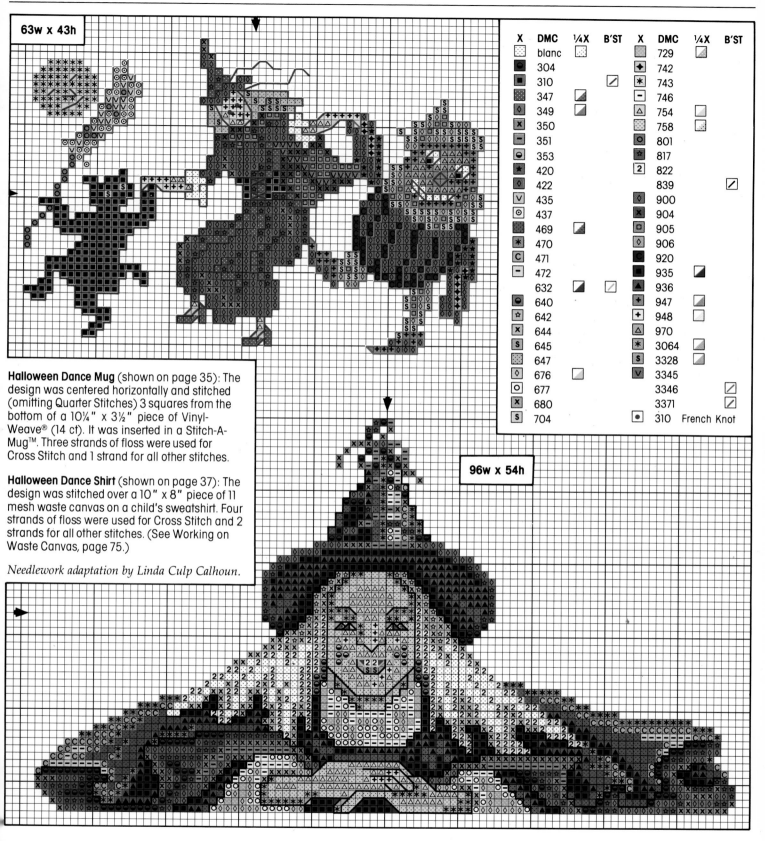

63w x 43h

X	DMC	¼X	B'ST		X	DMC	¼X	B'ST
	blanc					729		
	304					742		
	310		/			743		
	347	/			-	746		
	349	/				754		
	350					758		
	351					801		
	353					817		
	420				2	822		
	422					839		/
V	435					900		
	437					904		
	469	/				905		
	470					906		
C	471					920		
-	472					935		/
	632	/	/			936		
	640					947		/
	642					948		
	644					970		
S	645					3064		/
	647				S	3328		/
	676	/			V	3345		
	677					3346		/
	680					3371		/
S	704				●	310	French Knot	

Halloween Dance Mug (shown on page 35): The design was centered horizontally and stitched (omitting Quarter Stitches) 3 squares from the bottom of a 10¼" x 3½" piece of Vinyl-Weave® (14 ct). It was inserted in a Stitch-A-Mug™. Three strands of floss were used for Cross Stitch and 1 strand for all other stitches.

Halloween Dance Shirt (shown on page 37): The design was stitched over a 10" x 8" piece of 11 mesh waste canvas on a child's sweatshirt. Four strands of floss were used for Cross Stitch and 2 strands for all other stitches. (See Working on Waste Canvas, page 75.)

Needlework adaptation by Linda Culp Calhoun.

96w x 54h

Witch Basket Ornament (shown on page 35): The design was stitched on a 13" x 10" piece of Antique White Aida (14 ct). Three strands of floss were used for Cross Stitch and 1 strand for Backstitch.

For ornament, cut one 13" x 10" piece of Antique White Aida for backing. With right sides facing and leaving an opening at bottom edge for turning and stuffing, sew stitched piece and backing fabric together ¼" from edge of design. Leaving a ¼" seam allowance, cut out ornament; clip curves and turn right side out. Stuff with polyester fiberfill. Sew final closure by hand.

Refer to photo and hot glue ornament to edge of basket.

Needlework adaptation by Carol Emmer.

73

X	DMC	¼X	¾X	B'ST
	blanc			
■	310	◪	◪	◪
■	347	◪		
✱	349	◪		
C	350			
◇	420	◪		
✛	422	◪		
◆	433	◪		
☆	435			
⊙	437	◪		
△	645			
✕	647	◪		
	648		◪	
▦	704	◪	◪	*
−	726			
◆	741			
▦	742	◪		
S	743			
◉	754			
△	758			
V	780		◪	
✿	783	◪		
2	801			
■	817	◪		
▨	844	◪		
▨	869	◪		
★	895			
◇	905	◪		
✕	906			
▲	3345			
	3716	◪		
⊡	310	French Knot		

* Use 4 strands of floss for cat's eyes.

STITCH COUNT (71w x 49h)		
14 count	5⅛"	x 3½"
16 count	4½"	x 3⅛"
18 count	4"	x 2¾"
22 count	3¼"	x 2¼"

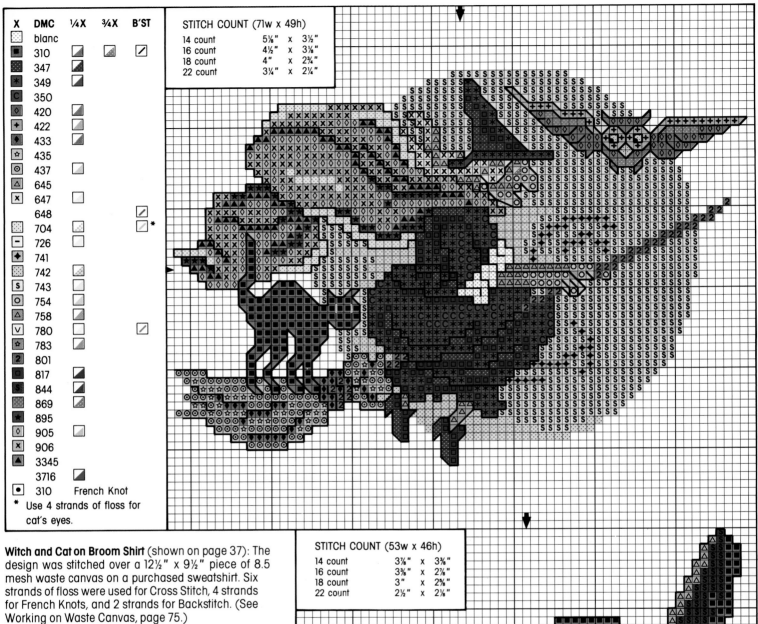

Witch and Cat on Broom Shirt (shown on page 37): The design was stitched over a 12½" x 9½" piece of 8.5 mesh waste canvas on a purchased sweatshirt. Six strands of floss were used for Cross Stitch, 4 strands for French Knots, and 2 strands for Backstitch. (See Working on Waste Canvas, page 75.)

Cat and Moon Shirt (shown on page 37): The design was stitched over a 10½" x 9" piece of 8.5 mesh waste canvas on a purchased sweatshirt. Six strands of floss were used for Cross Stitch and 2 strands for Backstitch. (See Working on Waste Canvas, page 75.)

For fence, cut one 6" length, one 7" length, and two 13" lengths of ⅞"w grosgrain ribbon. Press short ends of 13" lengths ¼" to wrong side. Press one short end of 6" and 7" lengths ¼" to wrong side. Fold each remaining short end to wrong side to form points; press. For each ribbon, cut a piece of paper-backed fusible web slightly smaller than ribbon; follow manufacturer's instructions to apply fusible web to wrong side of ribbon. Remove paper backing. Referring to photo, place 13" ribbon lengths horizontally on sweatshirt 1½" apart; fuse in place and topstitch close to all edges. Place remaining ribbon lengths vertically on sweatshirt; fuse in place and topstitch close to all edges.

Needlework adaptations by Linda Culp Calhoun.

STITCH COUNT (53w x 46h)		
14 count	3⅞"	x 3⅜"
16 count	3⅜"	x 2⅞"
18 count	3"	x 2⅝"
22 count	2½"	x 2⅛"

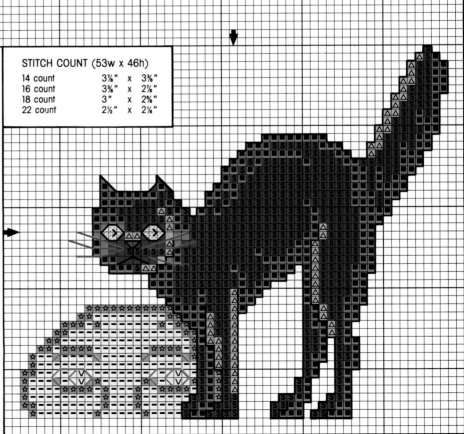

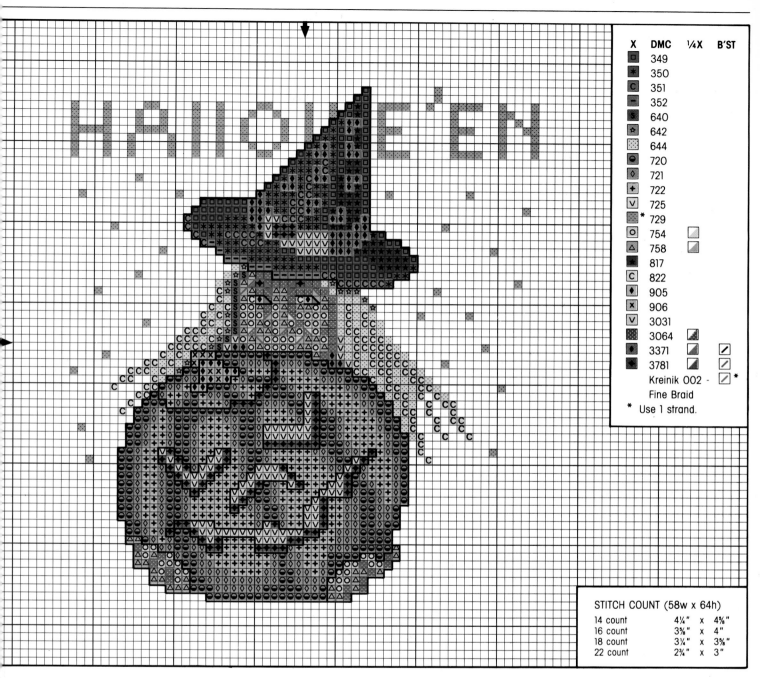

X	DMC	¼X	B'ST
☐	349		
✱	350		
C	351		
–	352		
S	640		
☆	642		
▦	644		
⊖	720		
◇	721		
+	722		
V	725		
▥ *	729		
O	754	◰	
△	758	◰	
■	817		
C	822		
◆	905		
X	906		
V	3031		
▨	3064	◰	
◆	3371	◰	◢
▓	3781	◰	◢
	Kreinik 002 -		◢ *
	Fine Braid		
*	Use 1 strand.		

STITCH COUNT (58w x 64h)

14 count	4¼"	x	4⅝"
16 count	3⅝"	x	4"
18 count	3¼"	x	3⅝"
22 count	2¾"	x	3"

Witch and Pumpkin Shirt (shown on page 36): The design was stitched over a 12" square of 5 mesh waste canvas on a purchased T-shirt. Six strands of floss were used for Cross Stitch (except where indicated on chart) and 2 strands for Backstitch. Gold 5mm star-shaped sequins and gold seed beads were added to shirt.

After waste canvas is removed, run needle threaded with 2 strands of DMC 729 up through center of each DMC 729 cross stitch. Thread sequin, then bead onto needle. Run thread back down through hole of sequin. Move to next cross stitch and continue adding sequins and beads .

Needlework adaptation by Carol Emmer.

WORKING ON WASTE CANVAS
Waste canvas is a special canvas that provides an evenweave grid for placing stitches on fabric. After the design is worked over the canvas, the canvas threads are removed leaving the design on the fabric. The canvas is available in several mesh sizes.

Cover edges of canvas with masking tape. Cut a piece of lightweight, non-fusible interfacing the same size as canvas to provide a firm stitching base.

Find desired stitching area on shirt and mark center of area with a pin. Match center of canvas to pin. Use the blue threads in canvas to place canvas straight on shirt; pin canvas to shirt. Pin interfacing to wrong side of shirt. Baste all three thicknesses together as shown in **Fig. 1**.

Place shirt in a screw type hoop. We recommend a hoop that is large enough to encircle entire design. Using a sharp needle, work design, stitching from large holes to large holes.

Trim canvas to within ¾" of design. Dampen canvas until it becomes limp. Pull out canvas threads one at a time using tweezers (**Fig. 2**). Trim interfacing close to design.

Fig. 1

Fig. 2

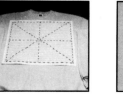

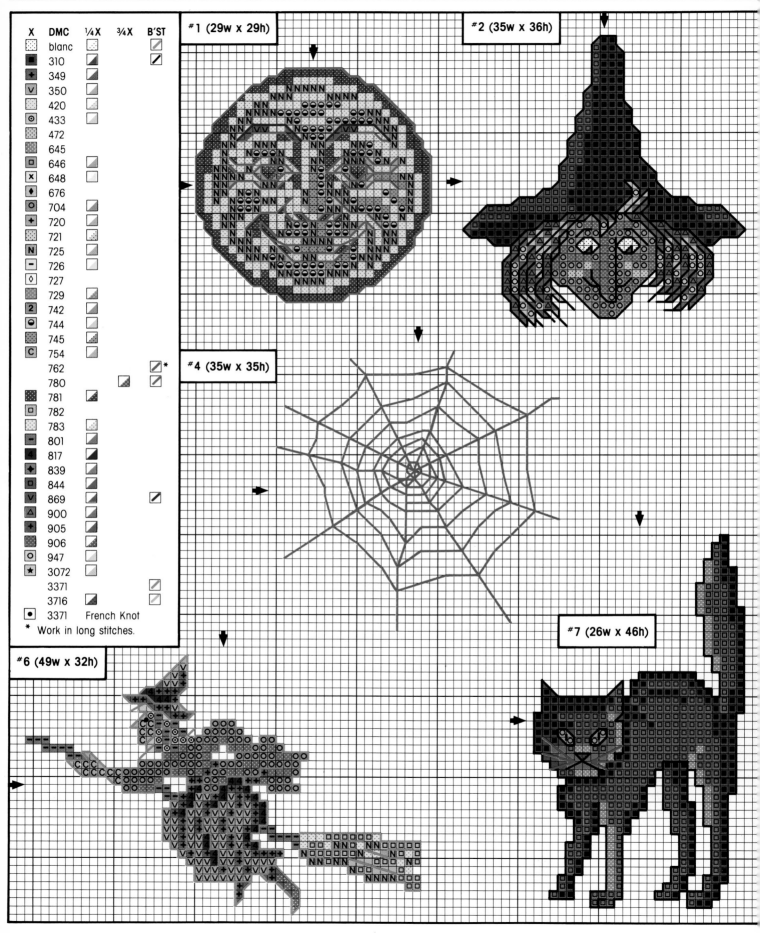

X	DMC	1/4X	3/4X	B'ST
	blanc			
	310			
	349			
V	350			
	420			
⊙	433			
	472			
	645			
□	646			
X	648			
◆	676			
O	704			
✦	720			
	721			
N	725			
−	726			
◇	727			
	729			
2	742			
⊖	744			
	745			
C	754			
	762			*
	780			
	781			
□	782			
	783			
⊟	801			
4	817			
✦	839			
□	844			
V	869			
△	900			
✚	905			
	906			
O	947			
★	3072			
	3371			
	3716			
●	3371	French Knot		

* Work in long stitches.

#1 (29w x 29h)

#2 (35w x 36h)

#4 (35w x 35h)

#6 (49w x 32h)

#7 (26w x 46h)

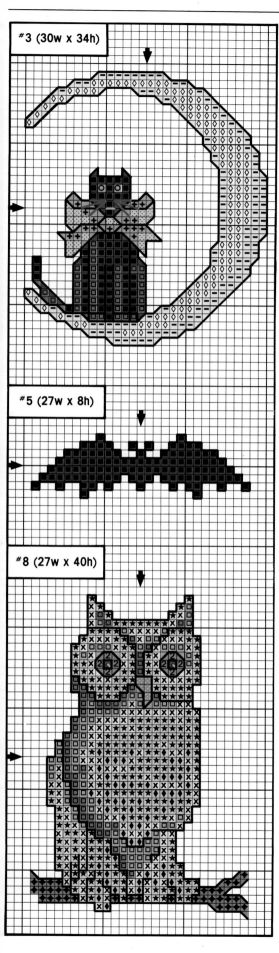

#3 (30w x 34h)

#5 (27w x 8h)

#8 (27w x 40h)

Moon Lapel Pin (shown on page 36): Design #1 was stitched on a 6" square of Ivory Aida (14 ct). Three strands of floss were used for Cross Stitch and 1 strand for Backstitch.

For stiffened lapel pin, cut one piece of cream medium weight fabric same size as stitched piece for backing. Apply a heavy coat of fabric stiffener to back of stitched piece using a small foam brush. Matching wrong sides, place stitched piece on backing fabric, smoothing stitched piece while pressing fabric pieces together; allow to dry. Apply fabric stiffener to backing fabric and allow to dry; repeat for front. Cut out close to edges of stitched design. Glue 1" pin back to back of stiffened piece.

Needlework adaptation by Nancy Dockter.

Witch Candy Bag (shown on page 35): Design #2 was stitched on a 6" square of Ivory Aida (14 ct). Three strands of floss were used for Cross Stitch and 1 strand for Backstitch. The design was stiffened and applied to a candy bag.

For candy bag, you will need fabric stiffener, small foam brush, 6" square of cream medium weight fabric for backing, two 5" x 6½" pieces of desired fabric for bag, one 18" length of ⅛"w ribbon, fabric glue, small safety pin, and liquid fray preventative.

For stiffened design, apply a heavy coat of fabric stiffener to back of stitched piece using foam brush. Matching wrong sides, place stitched piece on backing fabric smoothing stitched piece while pressing fabric pieces together; allow to dry. Apply fabric stiffener to backing fabric and allow to dry; repeat for front. Cut out close to edges of stitched design.

For candy bag, match right sides and raw edges and use a ¼" seam allowance to sew fabric pieces together along three sides, leaving one short side open. Turn raw edge of fabric ¼" to wrong side and press; turn edge ¼" to wrong side again and press. Topstitch close to first fold, making a ¼" casing. Trim seam allowances diagonally at corners and turn candy bag right side out. Cut a small opening in the back center of casing; apply liquid fray preventative to opening and allow to dry. For drawstring, thread ribbon through the center of small safety pin. Insert safety pin into hole in casing; carefully run pin through casing and out same hole. Remove safety pin from ribbon and apply liquid fray preventative to each end of ribbon. Referring to photo for placement, glue stiffened design to candy bag.

Cat on Moon Jar Lid (shown on page 35): Design #3 was stitched on a 6" square of Ivory Aida (14 ct). Three strands of floss were used for Cross Stitch and 1 strand for Backstitch. It was inserted in a large mouth jar lid.

For jar lid, use **outer edge** of jar lid for pattern and draw a circle on adhesive mounting board. Cutting slightly inside drawn line, cut out circle. Using **opening** of jar lid for pattern, cut a circle of batting. Remove paper from adhesive board; center batting on adhesive board and press in place. Center stitched piece on batting and press edges onto adhesive board; trim edges close to board. Glue board inside jar lid.

Spider Web Tie (shown on page 36): Design #4 was stitched over a 5½" square of 12 mesh waste canvas on a purchased tie. One strand of floss was used for design. (See Working on Waste Canvas below.)

Bat Socks (shown on page 36): Design #5 was stitched over a 4" x 3" piece of 14 mesh waste canvas on the cuffs of a pair of purchased socks. Three strands of floss were used for Cross Stitch and 1 strand for Backstitch. (See Working on Waste Canvas below.)

Needlework adaptations by Kathy Bradley.

Mini Pillow Ornaments (shown on page 35): Designs #6, #7, and #8 were each stitched on a 6" square of Ivory Aida (14 ct). Three strands of floss were used for Cross Stitch and 1 strand for Backstitch and French Knot.

For each ornament, cut stitched piece 1¼" larger than design on all sides. Cut one piece of Ivory Aida same size as stitched piece for backing.

With wrong sides facing, use desired floss color to cross stitch fabric pieces together ½" from bottom and side edges. Stuff with polyester fiberfill. Cross stitch across top of mini pillow ½" from edge. Fringe fabric to cross-stitched lines.

Needlework adaptations by Linda Culp Calhoun.

WORKING ON WASTE CANVAS
Cover edges of waste canvas with masking tape. Find desired stitching area and mark center of area with a pin. Match center of canvas to pin. Use the blue threads in canvas to place canvas straight on project; pin canvas to project. Baste canvas to project.

Using a sharp needle, work design, stitching from large holes to large holes. Trim canvas to within ¾" of design. Dampen canvas until it becomes limp. Pull out canvas threads one at a time using tweezers.

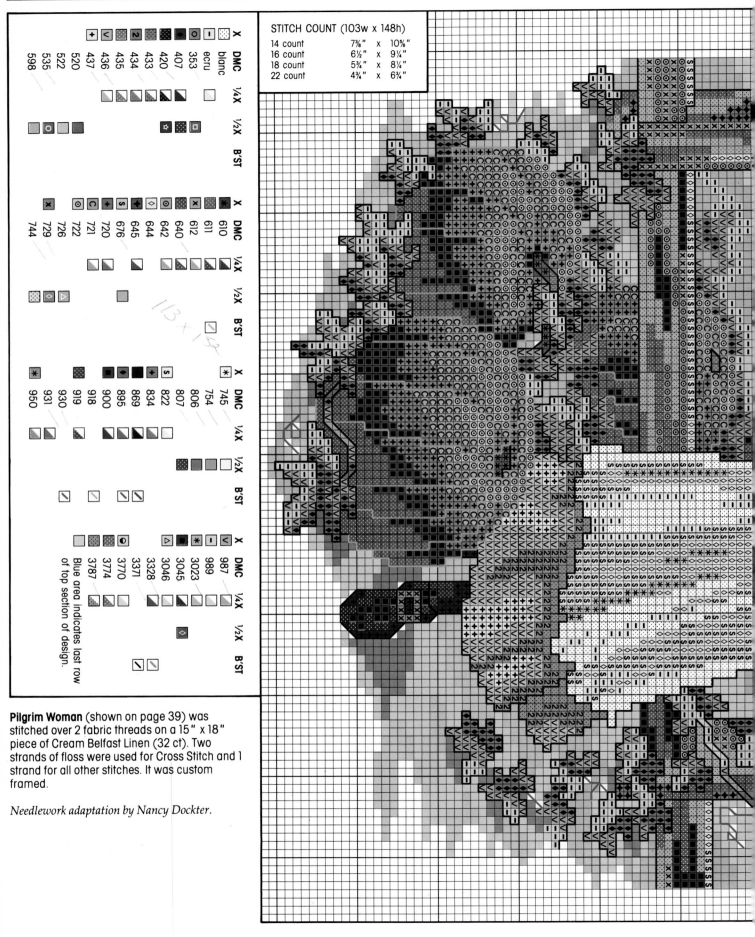

STITCH COUNT (103w x 148h)		
14 count	7⅜"	x 10⅝"
16 count	6½"	x 9¼"
18 count	5¾"	x 8¼"
22 count	4¾"	x 6¾"

Pilgrim Woman (shown on page 39) was stitched over 2 fabric threads on a 15" x 18" piece of Cream Belfast Linen (32 ct). Two strands of floss were used for Cross Stitch and 1 strand for all other stitches. It was custom framed.

Needlework adaptation by Nancy Dockter.

Blue area indicates last row of top section of design.

X	DMC	1/4X	1/2X	B'ST	X	DMC	1/4X	1/2X	B'ST	X	DMC	1/4X	1/2X	B'ST	X	DMC	1/4X	1/2X	B'ST	X	DMC	1/4X	1/2X	B'ST
	blanc				O	501					680					900				V	3781			
-	ecru				□	502				V	720					918			★					
	310					517				□	721				◆	919								
▲	311					518			†	⊙	725				□	930								
- *	311 &				◆	610					729				X	931								
	500					611				O	738					935								
	318				⊙	612				◊	739					937								
	351				☆ *	613 &				◆	741				■	938			†					
	352					677				*	742				☆	948								
⊙	407					632			★	+	746				△	950								
*	407 &					644				■	814				C	3022								
	950				⊙	645					815				2	3023								
V	415				+	647				⊙	816				4	3024								
3	420				C	676				X	839					3031								
*	437				△ *	676 &				▲	840					3078								
C	469					729					844			†	N	3371			★					
N	470				4 *	676 &				★	869					3778								
	500					744				+	898					3779								

* Use 1 strand of each floss color.

† Use 518 for eyes. Use 844 for woman's clothing. Use 938 for corn shocks and pumpkin stems.

★ Use 632 for faces and hands. Use 918 for pumpkins. Use 2 strands of 3371 for ship masts.

Puritan Relief Ship (shown on page 42): The design was stitched over 2 fabric threads on a 12" x 11" piece of Cream Belfast Linen (32 ct). Two strands of floss were used for Cross Stitch and 1 strand for all other stitches. It was custom framed.

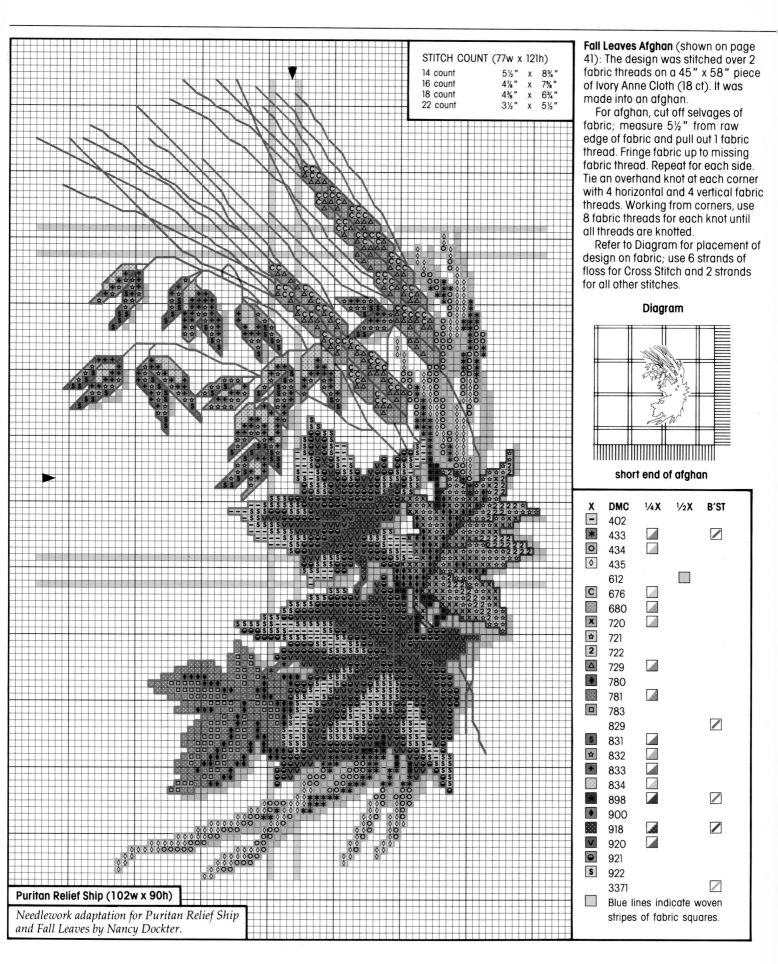

STITCH COUNT (77w x 121h)

14 count	5½"	x 8¾"
16 count	4⅞"	x 7⅝"
18 count	4⅜"	x 6¾"
22 count	3½"	x 5½"

Fall Leaves Afghan (shown on page 41): The design was stitched over 2 fabric threads on a 45" x 58" piece of Ivory Anne Cloth (18 ct). It was made into an afghan.

For afghan, cut off selvages of fabric; measure 5½" from raw edge of fabric and pull out 1 fabric thread. Fringe fabric up to missing fabric thread. Repeat for each side. Tie an overhand knot at each corner with 4 horizontal and 4 vertical fabric threads. Working from corners, use 8 fabric threads for each knot until all threads are knotted.

Refer to Diagram for placement of design on fabric; use 6 strands of floss for Cross Stitch and 2 strands for all other stitches.

Diagram

short end of afghan

X	DMC	¼X	½X	B'ST
–	402			
✳	433	◪		◪
○	434	◪		
◇	435			
	612		▨	
C	676	◪		
▨	680	◪		
X	720	◪		
☆	721			
2	722			
△	729	◪		
◆	780			
▨	781	◪		
▫	783			
	829			◪
S	831	◪		
☆	832	◪		
✚	833	◪		
▨	834	▨		
★	898	◪		◪
◆	900			
▨	918	◪		◪
V	920	◪		
◉	921			
S	922			
	3371			◪
▨	Blue lines indicate woven stripes of fabric squares.			

Puritan Relief Ship (102w x 90h)

Needlework adaptation for Puritan Relief Ship and Fall Leaves by Nancy Dockter.

81

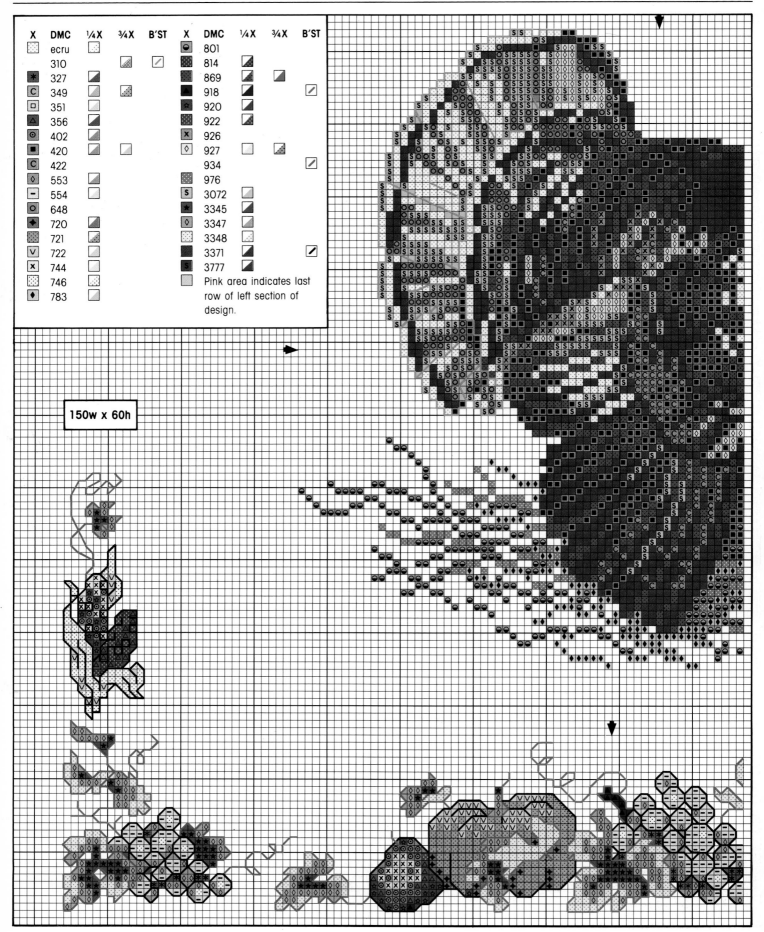

X	DMC	1/4 X	3/4 X	B'ST		X	DMC	1/4 X	3/4 X	B'ST
	ecru						801			
	310						814			
	327						869			
C	349						918			
	351						920			
	356						922			
	402					x	926			
	420						927			
C	422						934			
	553						976			
-	554					S	3072			
	648						3345			
	720						3347			
	721						3348			
V	722						3371			
x	744					S	3777			
	746									
	783						Pink area indicates last row of left section of design.			

150w x 60h

Thanksgiving Turkey Tray (shown on page 40): The design was stitched over 2 fabric threads on a 12" square of Cream Irish Linen (28 ct). Three strands of floss were used for Cross Stitch and 1 strand for Backstitch. It was inserted in a 12" x 9" purchased tray (10" x 7" oval opening).

Needlework adaptation by Mary Ellen Yanich.

Table Runner (shown on page 43): **Harvest Border** was centered horizontally and stitched across each short end of a piece of Cream Bantry Cloth (28 ct) with bottom of design 2" from raw edge of fabric. (Measure table to determine desired length of fabric.) The design was stitched over 2 fabric threads. Three strands of floss were used for Cross Stitch and 1 strand for Backstitch.

For table runner, machine stitch across each short edge of fabric ½" from raw edges. Fringe to machine-stitched line.

Breadcloth (shown on page 43): The center section of **Harvest Border** design (refer to photo) was stitched over 2 fabric threads on a 13½" x 20" piece of Cream Bantry Cloth (28 ct) with bottom of design 2" from raw edge of fabric. Three strands of floss were used for Cross Stitch and 1 strand for Backstitch.

For breadcloth, machine stitch across each short edge of fabric ½" from raw edges. Fringe to machine-stitched line.

Candle Band (shown on page 43): The grapes and leaves from center of **Harvest Border** design (refer to photo) were centered and stitched over 2 fabric threads on a 12" x 6" piece of Cream Bantry Cloth (28 ct). Three strands of floss were used for Cross Stitch and 1 strand for Backstitch. (**Note:** We used a candle measuring 2¾" in diameter. If using a different size candle, measurements for candle band will need to be adjusted.)

Matching right sides and long edges fold stitched piece in half. Using a ½" seam allowance, sew long edges together. Turn stitched piece right side out. Press flat with seam centered on back and design centered on front.

For cording, cut two 12" lengths of ⅛" dia. purchased cord and two 12" x 1¼" strips of Bantry Cloth. Center one length of purchased cord on one strip of fabric; matching raw edges, fold strip over cord. Using zipper foot, baste along length of strip close to cord. Repeat for remaining lengths of cord and fabric.

Referring to photo, topstitch one length of cording to each long edge of stitched piece. Turn each short end to back of stitched piece 1"; whipstitch in place. Wrap candle band around candle and whipstitch short ends together.

Napkin (shown on page 43): The grapes and leaves from left corner of **Harvest Border** design (refer to photo) were stitched over 2 fabric threads in corner of a 13½" square of Cream Bantry Cloth (28 ct) 1¾" from raw edges of fabric. Three strands of floss were used for Cross Stitch and 1 strand for Backstitch.

For napkin, trim selvages and machine stitch around fabric ½" from all edges. Fringe to machine-stitched lines.

Harvest Border designed by Jorja Hernandez, Kooler Design Studio.

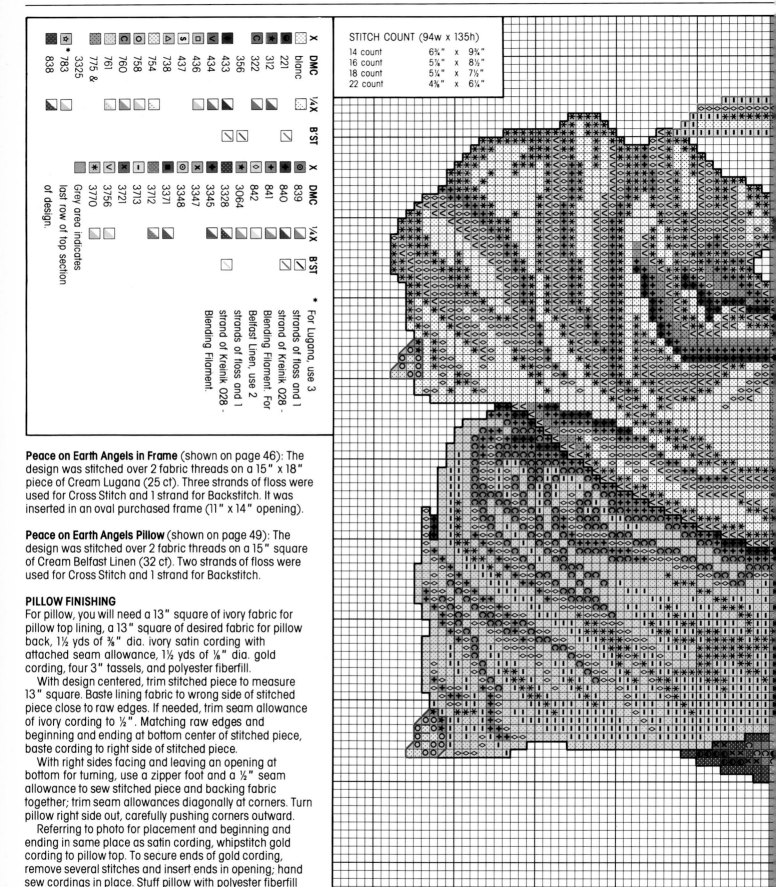

				STITCH COUNT (94w x 135h)		
				14 count	6¾"	x 9¾"
				16 count	5⅞"	x 8½"
				18 count	5¼"	x 7½"
				22 count	4⅜"	x 6¼"

Key (first block)

X	¼X	B'ST	DMC
			blanc
			221
			312
			322
			356
			433
			434
			436
			437
			438
			754
			758
			760
			761
			775 &
			3325
			*783
			838

Key (second block)

X	¼X	B'ST	DMC
			839
			840
			841
			842
			3064
			3328
			3345
			3347
			3348
			3371
			3712
			3713
			3721
			3756
			3770

* For Lugana, use 3 strands of floss and 1 strand of Kreinik 028 - Blending Filament. For Belfast Linen, use 2 strands of floss and 1 strand of Kreinik 028 - Blending Filament.

Grey area indicates last row of top section of design.

Peace on Earth Angels in Frame (shown on page 46): The design was stitched over 2 fabric threads on a 15" x 18" piece of Cream Lugana (25 ct). Three strands of floss were used for Cross Stitch and 1 strand for Backstitch. It was inserted in an oval purchased frame (11" x 14" opening).

Peace on Earth Angels Pillow (shown on page 49): The design was stitched over 2 fabric threads on a 15" square of Cream Belfast Linen (32 ct). Two strands of floss were used for Cross Stitch and 1 strand for Backstitch.

PILLOW FINISHING

For pillow, you will need a 13" square of ivory fabric for pillow top lining, a 13" square of desired fabric for pillow back, 1½ yds of ⅜" dia. ivory satin cording with attached seam allowance, 1½ yds of ⅛" dia. gold cording, four 3" tassels, and polyester fiberfill.

With design centered, trim stitched piece to measure 13" square. Baste lining fabric to wrong side of stitched piece close to raw edges. If needed, trim seam allowance of ivory cording to ½". Matching raw edges and beginning and ending at bottom center of stitched piece, baste cording to right side of stitched piece.

With right sides facing and leaving an opening at bottom for turning, use a zipper foot and a ½" seam allowance to sew stitched piece and backing fabric together; trim seam allowances diagonally at corners. Turn pillow right side out, carefully pushing corners outward.

Referring to photo for placement and beginning and ending in same place as satin cording, whipstitch gold cording to pillow top. To secure ends of gold cording, remove several stitches and insert ends in opening; hand sew cordings in place. Stuff pillow with polyester fiberfill and sew final closure by hand. Sew tassel to each corner.

Needlework adaptation by Carol Emmer.

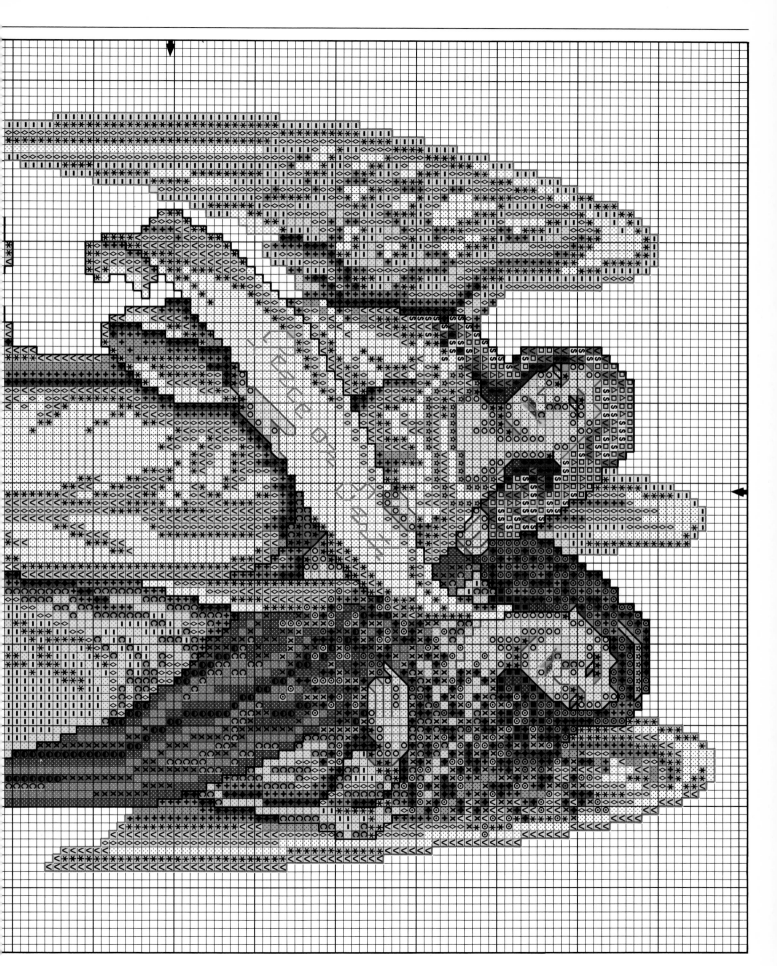

Christmas

Angel Ornaments (shown on pages 44-45): The designs were each stitched over 2 fabric threads on a 7" x 9" piece of Cream Irish Linen (36 ct). Two strands of floss were used for Cross Stitch and 1 strand for Backstitch. They were made into ornaments.

For each ornament, you will need tracing paper, 7" x 9" piece of Cream Irish Linen for backing fabric, 10" x 7" piece of adhesive board, 10" x 7" piece of batting, 18" length of ¼" dia. ivory satin cording with attached seam allowance, 18" length of ⅜"w gold trim, 3" tassel, 14" length of ½"w gold wire-edged ribbon, and 6½" length of ⅛" dia. gold cording for hanger.

Trace oval pattern (page 92) onto tracing paper; cut out pattern. Draw around pattern twice on adhesive board and twice on batting; cut out. Remove paper from adhesive board and stick one batting piece on each adhesive board piece.

Center oval pattern over stitched piece; pin in place. Cut out stitched piece ½" larger than pattern on all sides; remove pattern. Cut out backing fabric same size as stitched piece. Center stitched piece right side up on top of batting; smoothly fold and glue edges to back of board clipping into edges of fabric as needed. Repeat with backing fabric and remaining adhesive board piece for ornament back.

Glue cording seam allowance to wrong side of ornament front beginning at bottom of oval. Glue ends of cording to wrong side of ornament front and trim ends if needed. Referring to photo for placement, glue ⅜"w trim to back of ornament front beginning at bottom of oval. Overlap ends and trim if needed. Glue tassel to wrong side of ornament front at bottom of oval. For hanger, glue ends of gold cording to wrong side of ornament front at top of oval.

Glue wrong sides of ornament front and back together. Weight with a heavy book until glue is dry. Tie wire-edged ribbon in a bow and glue to bottom of ornament; trim ends as desired.

Needlework adaptation by Carol Emmer.

Angel Porcelain Jar (shown on page 48): The design was stitched over 2 fabric threads on an 8" square of Cream Belfast Linen (32 ct). Two strands of floss were used for Cross Stitch and 1 strand for Backstitch. It was inserted in the lid of a 5" dia. porcelain jar (3½" dia. opening).

Designed by Carol Emmer.

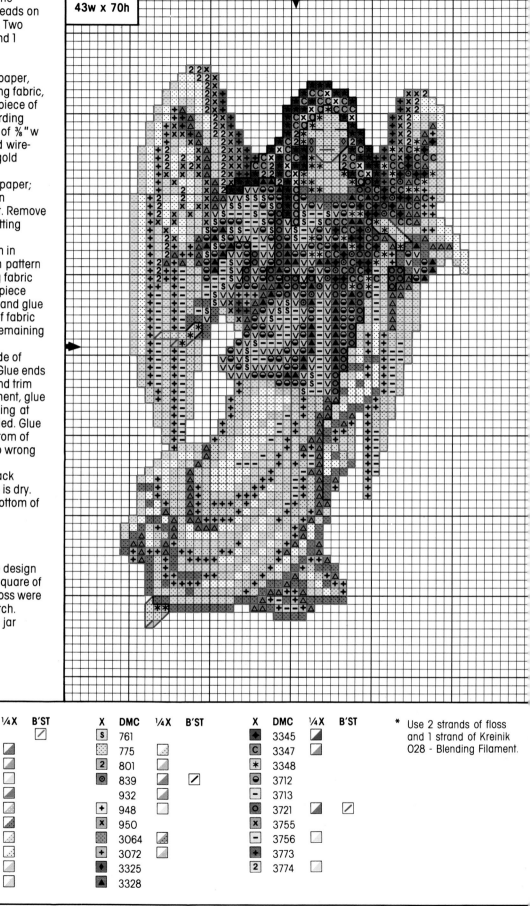

43w x 70h

X	DMC	¼X	B'ST		X	DMC	¼X	B'ST		S	DMC	¼X	B'ST		X	DMC	¼X	B'ST	
	blanc					647		✓		S	761				+	3345			
■	322	◨			△	648	◨				775				C	3347	◨		
◆	353	◨			⊙	676	◨			2	801	◨			*	3348			
	356		✓		S	677	◨			⊙	839	◨	✓		⊙	3712	◨		
▣	420		✓		▲	680	◨				932	◨			-	3713			
■	433	◨				729	◨			+	948				◉	3721	◨	✓	
C	434		✓		*	729	◨			x	950				X	3755			
S	435	◨				746					3064	◨			-	3756			
x	436					754				+	3072	◨				3773			
○	437				*	758	◨			◆	3325				2	3774			
	646		✓		V	760				▲	3328								

* Use 2 strands of floss and 1 strand of Kreinik 028 - Blending Filament.

86

38w x 71h

43w x 67h

42w x 34h

Christmas

Gloria Angel Stocking (shown on page 47): The design was stitched over 2 fabric threads on a 17" x 21" piece of Cream Lugana (25 ct) with top of design 8" from one short edge of fabric. Three strands of floss were used for Cross Stitch and 1 strand for Backstitch. (See Stocking Finishing, page 90.)

Gloria Angel Pillow (shown on page 49): The design was stitched over 2 fabric threads on a 10" x 14" piece of Cream Irish Linen (36 ct). Two strands of floss were used for Cross Stitch and 1 strand for Backstitch. It was applied to a custom made pillow. (See Pillow Finishing below.)

PILLOW FINISHING

For pillow, you will need, a 7½" x 11½" piece of ivory fabric for lining stitched piece, two 3¼" x 11½" strips of ivory fabric, two 17" x 11½" pieces of fabric for pillow front and back, 1⅔ yds of ½" dia. purchased cord, 2½" x 1⅔ yds bias strip of fabric for cording, polyester fiberfill, and two 11½" lengths of each of the following: ¼" dia. ivory satin cording with attached seam allowance, ⅞"w gold trim, and ⅜"w gold trim.

    With design centered, trim stitched piece to measure 7½" x 11½". Baste lining fabric to back of stitched piece close to raw edges. If needed, trim seam allowance of ¼" dia. satin cording to ½". Matching raw edges, baste one length of satin cording to right side of stitched piece along one long edge. Repeat for remaining length of cording and long edge of stitched piece.

    Matching wrong sides and long edges fold each 3¼" x 11½" fabric strip in half; press. Matching raw edges, lay one folded fabric strip over cording on top of stitched piece and baste together. Repeat for remaining long edge of stitched piece and fabric strip. Using zipper foot and ½" seam allowance, sew cording and fabric strip to each side of stitched piece. Press seam allowances toward stitched piece. Referring to photo for placement, hand sew ⅜"w trim to folded edge of each fabric strip.

    For pillow front, center stitched piece right side up on right side of one 17" x 11½" piece of fabric; pin in place. To attach stitched piece to pillow top, sew along center of each fabric strip through all thicknesses.

    For fabric cording, center purchased cord on wrong side of bias fabric strip. Matching long edges, fold strip over cord. Using zipper foot, baste along length of strip close to cord; trim seam allowance to ½".

    Matching raw edges and beginning at bottom center, pin cording to right side of pillow front making a ⅜" clip in seam allowance of cording at each corner. Ends of cording should overlap approximately 2"; pin overlapping end out of the way. Starting 2" from beginning end of cording and ending 4" from overlapping end, baste cording to pillow front. On overlapping end of cording, remove 2½" of basting; fold end of fabric back and trim cord so that it meets beginning end of cord. Fold end of fabric under ½"; wrap fabric over beginning end of cording. Finish basting cording to pillow front.

    Matching right sides and raw edges, use a ½" seam allowance to sew pillow front and backing fabric together leaving an opening for turning and stuffing. Trim seam allowances diagonally at corners and turn pillow right side out, carefully pushing corners outward. Stuff pillow with polyester fiberfill and whipstitch opening closed.

    Referring to photo for placement, hand sew one length of ⅞"w trim to each fabric strip covering stitching line.

Needlework adaptation by Carol Emmer.

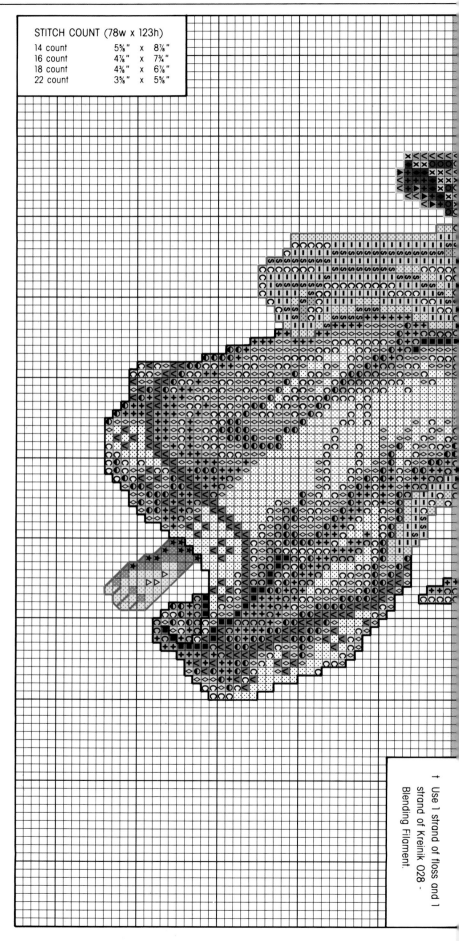

STITCH COUNT (78w x 123h)

14 count	5⅝"	x 8⅞"
16 count	4⅞"	x 7¾"
18 count	4⅜"	x 6⅞"
22 count	3⅝"	x 5⅝"

† Use 1 strand of floss and 1 strand of Kreinik 028 - Blending Filament.

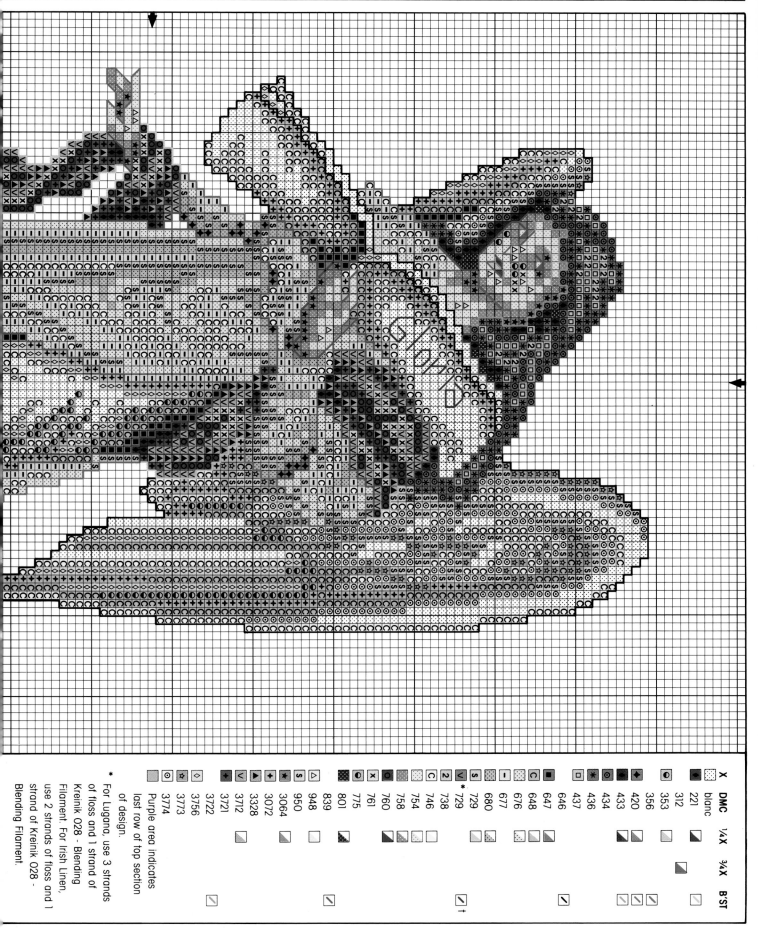

Evergreen Angel Stocking (shown on page 47): The design was stitched over 2 fabric threads on a 17" x 21" piece of Cream Lugana (25 ct) with top of design 8" from one short edge of fabric. Three strands of floss were used for Cross Stitch and 1 strand for Backstitch. (See Stocking Finishing below.)

Evergreen Angel Pillow (shown on page 48): The design was stitched over 2 fabric threads on a 10" x 14" piece of Cream Irish Linen (36 ct). Two strands of floss were used for Cross Stitch and 1 strand for Backstitch. It was applied to a custom made pillow. (See Pillow Finishing, page 88.)

STOCKING FINISHING

For stocking , you will need a 17" x 21" piece of Cream Lugana for backing, two 17" x 21" pieces of ivory fabric for lining, a 16" x 10" piece of coordinating fabric for cuff, 36" length of ¼" dia. ivory satin cording with attached seam allowance, 36" length of ⅛" dia. gold cording, 24" length of 1½"w satin ribbon, and 20" length of gold double tasseled cord.

Matching arrows to form one pattern, trace entire stocking pattern (page 92) onto tracing paper; cut out pattern. Matching right sides and raw edges, place stitched piece and backing fabric together. Place pattern on wrong side of stitched piece. Referring to photo for placement, position pattern on design; pin pattern in place. Cut out fabric pieces ½" larger than pattern on all sides. Remove pattern.

Place pieces of lining fabric together. Draw around pattern and sew lining pieces together around sides and bottom just inside drawn line. Trim top edge along drawn line. Trim seam allowance close to stitching. **Do not turn lining right side out.** Press top edge of lining ½" to wrong side.

If needed, trim seam allowance of ivory cording to ½". Matching raw edges and beginning 3" from top of one side of stocking, baste cording to right side of stitched piece, ending 3" from top of other side of stocking. Referring to photo for placement and beginning and ending in same place as satin cording, whipstitch gold cording to stocking front.

With right sides facing and leaving top edge open, use a zipper foot and a ½" seam allowance to sew stocking front and back together; clip seam allowances at curves. Turn stocking right side out.

Matching right sides and short edges of cuff fabric, use a ½" seam allowance to sew short edges together. Matching wrong sides and raw edges, fold cuff in half and press. Matching raw edges, place cuff inside stocking with cuff seam at center back of stocking. Use a ½" seam allowance to sew cuff and stocking together. Fold cuff 4" over stocking and press.

With wrong sides facing, place lining inside stocking; whipstitch lining to stocking.

Tie satin ribbon in a bow; trim ends as desired. Tie tasseled cord in a bow around knot of satin bow. Referring to photo, tack bows to cuff of stocking.

Needlework adaptation by Carol Emmer.

STITCH COUNT (73w x 121h)

14 count	5¼"	x	8¾"
16 count	4⅝"	x	7⅝"
18 count	4⅛"	x	6¾"
22 count	3⅜"	x	5½"

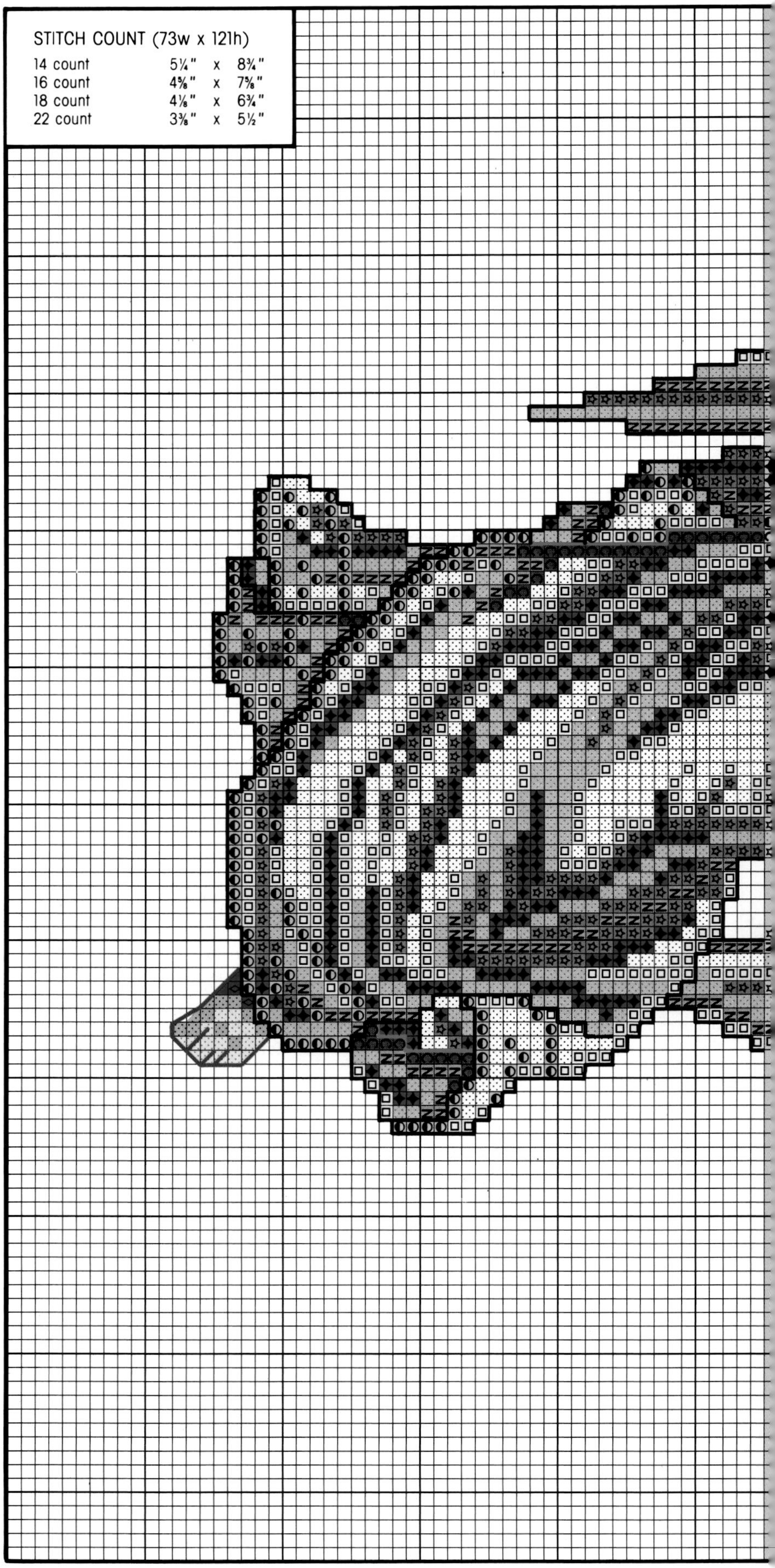

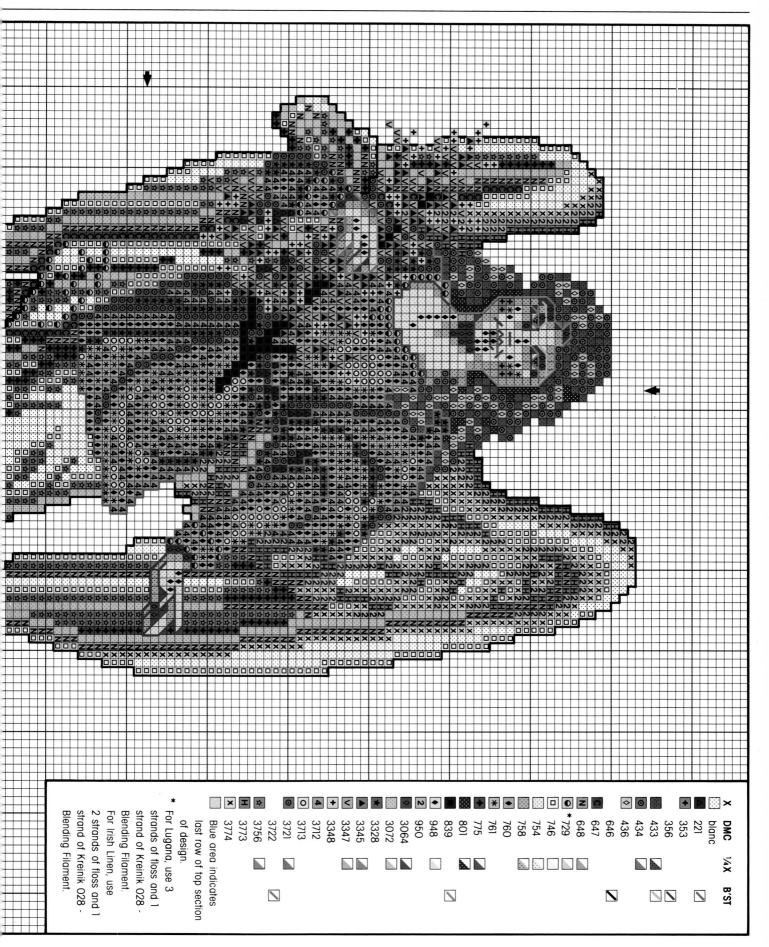

Christmas

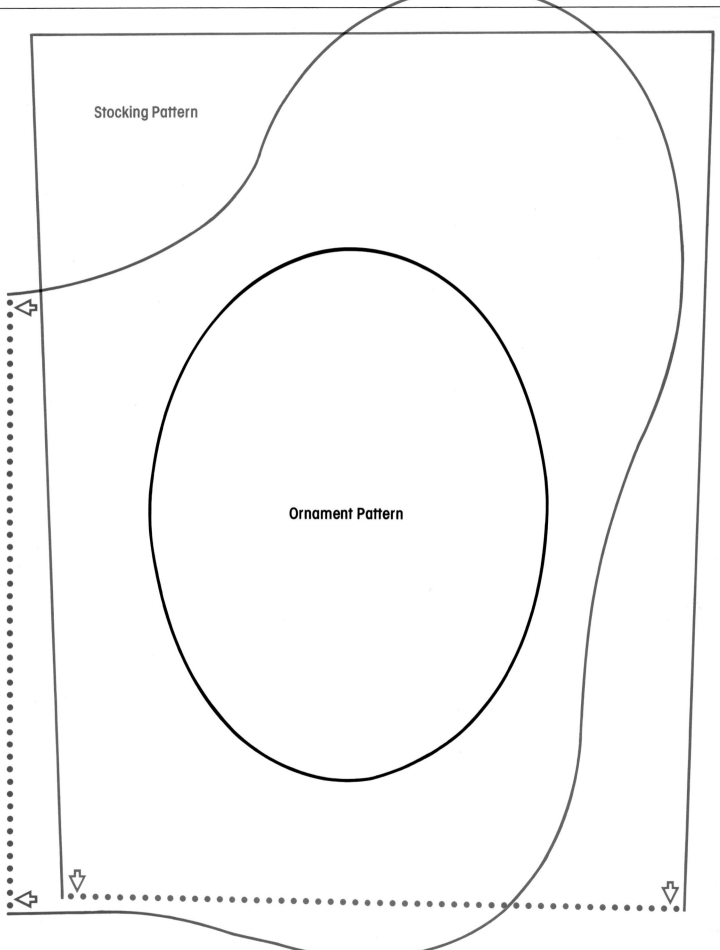

Stocking Pattern

Ornament Pattern

may day

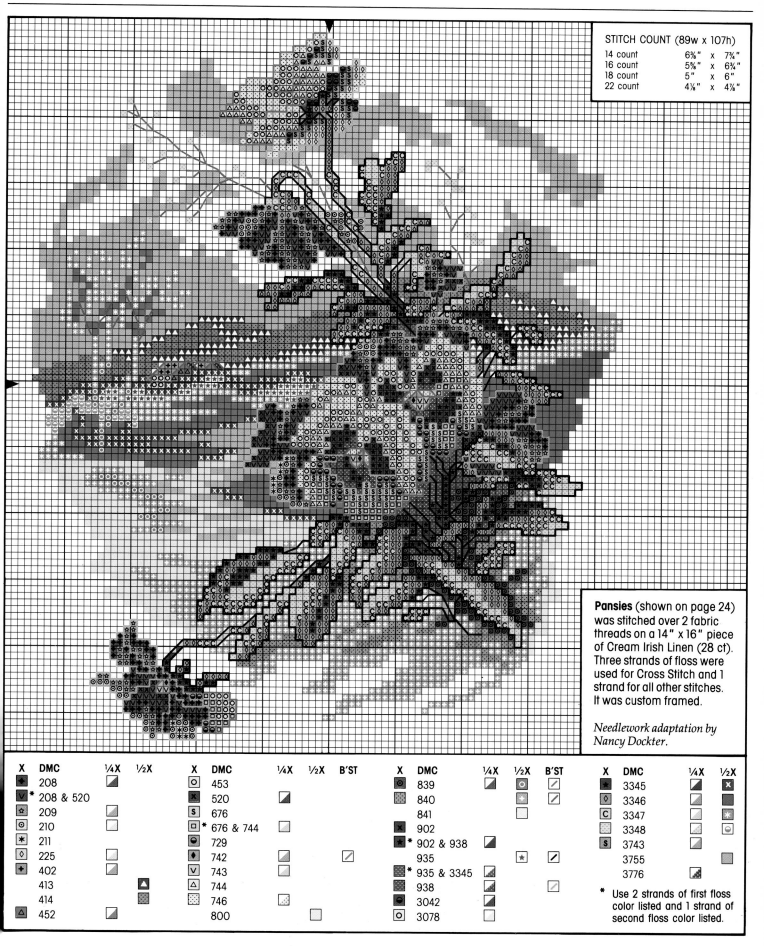

STITCH COUNT (89w x 107h)

14 count	6⅜"	x	7¾"
16 count	5⅝"	x	6¾"
18 count	5"	x	6"
22 count	4⅛"	x	4⅞"

Pansies (shown on page 24) was stitched over 2 fabric threads on a 14" x 16" piece of Cream Irish Linen (28 ct). Three strands of floss were used for Cross Stitch and 1 strand for all other stitches. It was custom framed.

Needlework adaptation by Nancy Dockter.

X	DMC	¼X	½X		X	DMC	¼X	½X	B'ST		X	DMC	¼X	½X	B'ST		X	DMC	¼X	½X
✦	208	◩			⊙	453					⊡	839	◩	⊙	⊘		★	3345	◩	⊠
V*	208 & 520				✖	520	◩				▒	840		✦	⊘		◇	3346	◩	◆
☆	209	◩			S	676						841		□			C	3347	◩	★
⊙	210	□			⊡*	676 & 744	◩				✖	902					▒	3348	□	⊙
✶	211				◐	729					★*	902 & 938	◩				S	3743		◩
◇	225	□			◆	742	◩		⊘			935		★	⊘			3755		□
✦	402	◩			V	743	◩				▒*	935 & 3345	◩					3776	◪	
	413		▲		△	744	◩				▒	938	◩		⊘					
	414		▒		▒	746	□				◐	3042	◩							
△	452	◩				800		□			⊙	3078	□							

* Use 2 strands of first floss color listed and 1 strand of second floss color listed.

93

May Day

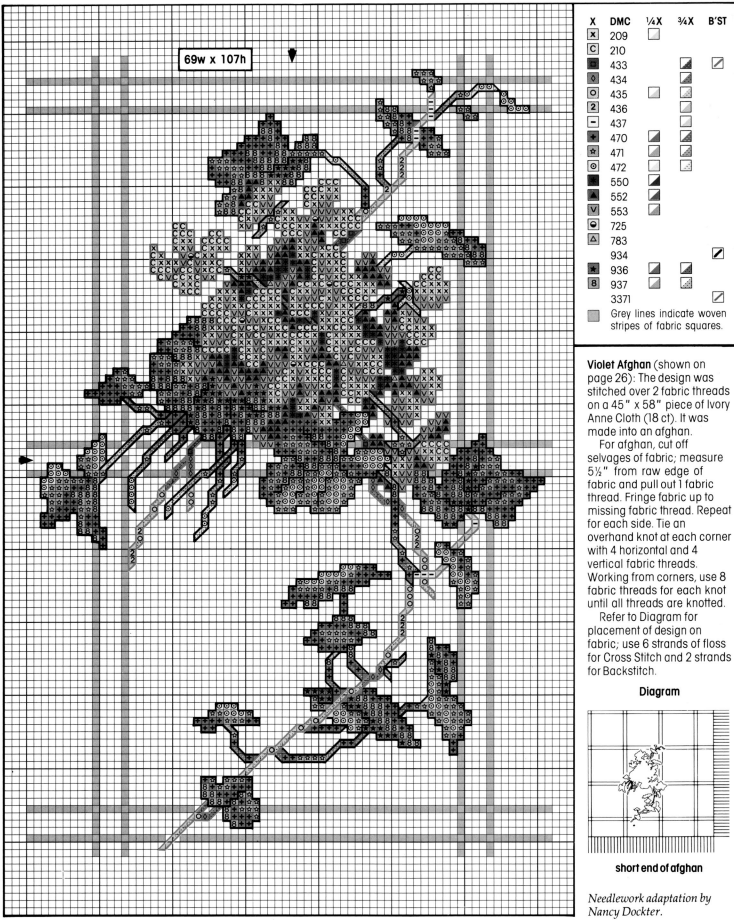

X	DMC	¼X	¾X	B'ST
x	209	◩		
C	210			
■	433		◩	◩
◊	434		◩	
O	435	◩	◩	
2	436		◩	
-	437		◩	
+	470	◩	◩	
☆	471	◩	◩	
⊙	472	◩	◩	
✱	550	◩		
▲	552	◩		
V	553	◩		
◓	725			
△	783			
	934			◩
★	936	◩	◩	
8	937	◩	◩	
	3371			◩
▒	Grey lines indicate woven stripes of fabric squares.			

Violet Afghan (shown on page 26): The design was stitched over 2 fabric threads on a 45" x 58" piece of Ivory Anne Cloth (18 ct). It was made into an afghan.

For afghan, cut off selvages of fabric; measure 5½" from raw edge of fabric and pull out 1 fabric thread. Fringe fabric up to missing fabric thread. Repeat for each side. Tie an overhand knot at each corner with 4 horizontal and 4 vertical fabric threads. Working from corners, use 8 fabric threads for each knot until all threads are knotted.

Refer to Diagram for placement of design on fabric; use 6 strands of floss for Cross Stitch and 2 strands for Backstitch.

Diagram

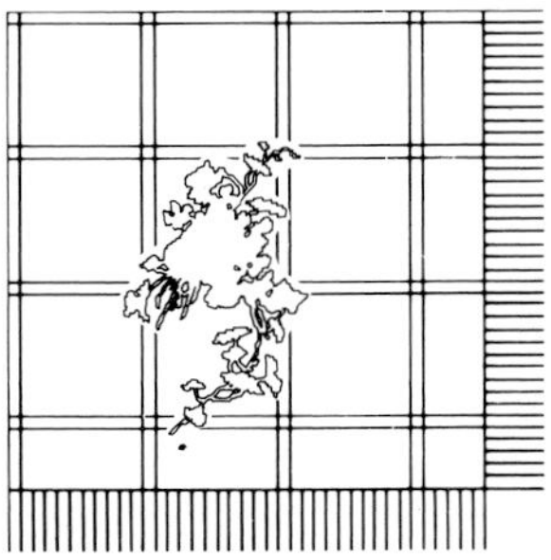

short end of afghan

Needlework adaptation by Nancy Dockter.

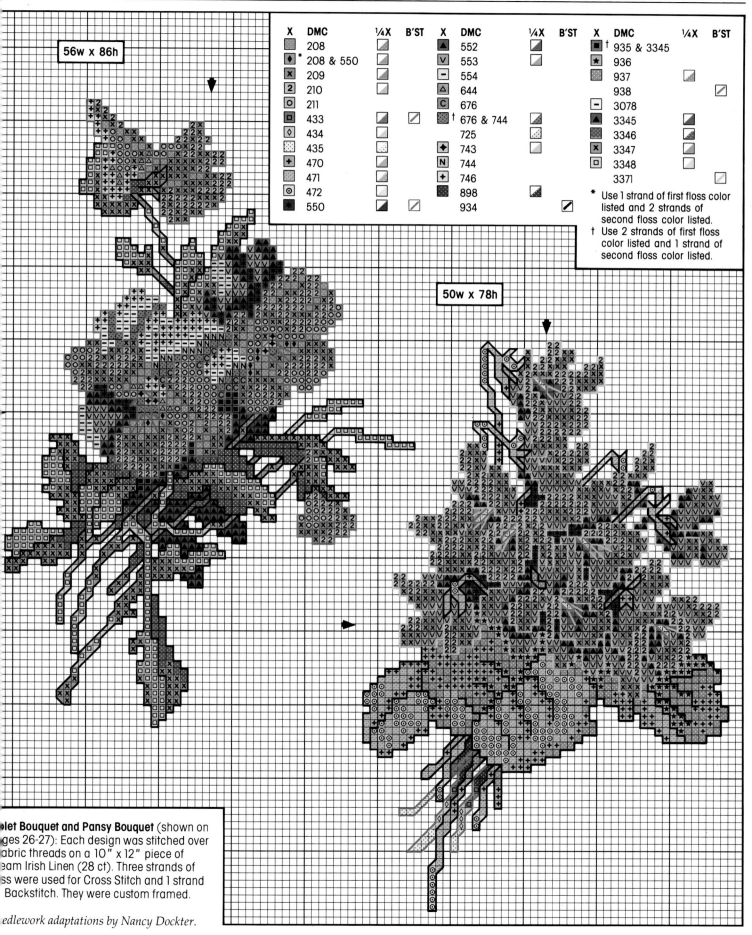

56w x 86h

X	DMC	¼X	B'ST	X	DMC	¼X	B'ST	X	DMC	¼X	B'ST
	208			▲	552			■ †	935 & 3345		
♦ *	208 & 550			V	553			★	936		
✕	209			−	554				937		
2	210			△	644				938		
⊙	211			C	676			−	3078		
⊡	433			†	676 & 744			▲	3345		
◇	434				725				3346		
	435			♦	743			✕	3347		
✚	470			N	744			⊡	3348		
	471			✚	746				3371		
⊙	472				898						
✳	550				934						

* Use 1 strand of first floss color listed and 2 strands of second floss color listed.

† Use 2 strands of first floss color listed and 1 strand of second floss color listed.

50w x 78h

let Bouquet and Pansy Bouquet (shown on
ges 26-27): Each design was stitched over
abric threads on a 10" x 12" piece of
eam Irish Linen (28 ct). Three strands of
ss were used for Cross Stitch and 1 strand
Backstitch. They were custom framed.

edlework adaptations by Nancy Dockter.

GENERAL INSTRUCTIONS

WORKING WITH CHARTS

How to Read Charts: Each of the designs is shown in chart form. Each colored square on the chart represents one Cross Stitch or one Half Cross Stitch. Each colored triangle on the chart represents one One-Quarter Stitch or one Three-Quarter Stitch. Black or colored dots represent French Knots. Colored ovals represent Lazy Daisy Stitches. The black or colored straight lines on the chart indicate Backstitch. When a French Knot, Lazy Daisy Stitch, or Backstitch covers a square, the symbol is omitted.

Each chart is accompanied by a color key. This key indicates the color of floss to use for each stitch on the chart. The headings on the color key are for Cross Stitch (**X**), DMC color number (**DMC**), Quarter Stitch (**¼X**), Three-Quarter Stitch (**¾X**), Half Cross Stitch (**½X**), and Backstitch (**B'ST**). Color key columns should be read vertically and horizontally to determine type of stitch and floss color.

Where to Start: The horizontal and vertical centers of each charted design are shown by arrows. You may start at any point on the charted design, but be sure the design will be centered on the fabric. Locate the center of fabric by folding in half, top to bottom and again left to right. On the charted design, count the number of squares (stitches) from the center of the chart to where you wish to start. Then from the fabric's center, find your starting point by counting out the same number of fabric threads (stitches).

STITCH DIAGRAMS

Counted Cross Stitch (X): Work one Cross Stitch to correspond to each colored square on the chart. For horizontal rows, work stitches in two journeys (**Fig. 1**). For vertical rows, complete each stitch as shown (**Fig. 2**). When working over two fabric threads, work Cross Stitch as shown in **Fig. 3**. When the chart shows a Backstitch crossing a colored square (**Fig. 4**), a Cross Stitch should be worked first; then the Backstitch (**Fig. 9 or 10**) should be worked on top of the Cross Stitch.

Fig. 1

Fig. 2

Fig. 3

Fig. 4

Quarter Stitch (¼X and ¾X): Quarter Stitches are denoted by triangular shapes of color on the chart and on the color key. Come up at 1 (**Fig. 5**); then split fabric thread to go down at 2. When stitches 1-4 are worked in the same color, the resulting stitch is called a Three-Quarter Stitch (**¾X**). **Fig. 6** shows the technique for Quarter Stitches when working over two fabric threads.

Fig. 5

Fig. 6

Half Cross Stitch (½X): This stitch is one journey of the Cross Stitch and is worked from lower left to upper right as shown in **Fig. 7**. When working over two fabric threads, work Half Cross Stitch as shown in **Fig. 8**.

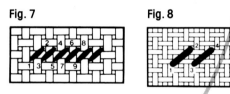

Fig. 7

Fig. 8

Backstitch (B'ST): For outline detail, Backstitch (shown on chart and on color key by black or colored straight lines) should be worked after the design has been completed (**Fig. 9**). When working over two fabric threads, work Backstitch as shown in **Fig. 10**.

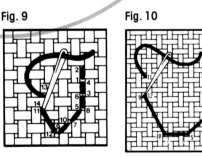

Fig. 9

Fig. 10

French Knot: Bring needle up at 1. Wrap floss once around needle and insert needle at 2, holding end of floss with non-stitching fingers (**Fig. 11**). Tighten knot; then pull needle through fabric, holding floss until it must be released. For larger knot, use more strands; wrap only once.

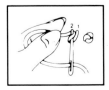

Fig. 11

Lazy Daisy Stitch: Bring needle up at 1 and make a loop. Go down at 1 and come up at 2, keeping floss below point of needle (**Fig. 12**). Pull needle through and go down at 2 to anchor loop, completing stitch. (**Note:** To support stitches, it may be helpful to go down in edge of next fabric thread when anchoring loop.)

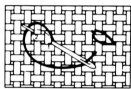

Fig. 12

STITCHING TIP

Working Over Two Fabric Threads: Use the sewing method instead of the stab method when working over two fabric threads. To use the sewing method, keep your stitching hand on the right side of the fabric (instead of stabbing the fabric with the needle and taking your stitching hand to the back of the fabric to pick up the needle). With the sewing method, you take the needle down and up with one stroke instead of two. To add support to stitches, it is important that the first Cross Stitch is placed on the fabric with stitch 1-2 beginning and ending where a vertical fabric thread crosses over a horizontal fabric thread (**Fig. 13**). When the first stitch is in the correct position, the entire design will be placed properly, with vertical fabric threads supporting each stitch.

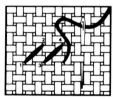

Fig. 13

Instructions tested and photo items made by Vicky Bishop, Anne Coppenger, Anita Drennan, Marilyn Fendley, Karen Foster, Joyce Graves, Muriel Hicks, Barbara Hodges, Ginny Hogue, Kathy Kampbell, Susan McDonald, Jill Morgan, Martha Nolan, Wesley Nuckolls, Ray Ellen Odle, Gail O'Nale, Mary Phinney, Susan Sego, Karen Sisco, Debra Smith, Amy Taylor, Michelle Tedder, Karen Tyler, Patricia Vines, Jane Walker, Karey Weeks, Andrea Westbrook, and Marie Williford.